LITTLE POEMS
about
BIG IDEAS
in
SCIENCE

ALBERT J. MUSMANNO SR.

iUniverse, Inc.
Bloomington

Little poems about Big Ideas in Science

iUniverse books may be ordered through booksellers or by contacting:

iUniverse
1663 Liberty Drive
Bloomington, IN 47403
www.iuniverse.com
1-800-Authors (1-800-288-4677)

ISBN: 978-1-4759-3988-0 (sc)
ISBN: 978-1-4759-3989-7 (e)

Library of Congress Control Number: 2012913364

Printed in the United States of America

iUniverse rev. date: 8/31/2012

Al Musmanno invites you to enjoy learning the important science education involved in the Science core Curriculum Content Standards from the state and the National Science Content Standards from the National Science Teachers Association. The poems will be easy to learn because they rhyme. For example, you will learn what an insect is from the grasshopper poem. The chorus to the poem goes " I am an insect. I've got six legs you see. And Three parts of my body- I am an insect.

The "magic of rhyme " will make learning easier most of the time. Many years ago, when I first started teaching, I was told that the principal would be coming in to evaluate my lesson on Monday. I was worried and wanted to do my best. We were studying the cell and the vocabulary included the words—endoplasmic reticulum—mitochondrion – vacuole. A lot of my students had trouble reading so I had to develop an easier way for them to learn. I was a lead singer in a band in my younger years and realized that the rhymes to the songs made it easy for me to remember So I wrote my first Science poem and Science song – The Cell –. I drew the parts of the cell on the board, labeled them and then told them what the parts did. The students copied the drawing Then as a review of the lesson we read the cell poem. The kids loved it and my principal thought it was a great lesson.

Use the poems in my book to sauce up your lessons in science. I even invited my students to write science poems about the science topics we were studying. They even wrote science songs. I taught for 41 years using my poems and songs about science to stir up the "magic of rhyme" in my classroom and to stir up the learning of my students. I even taught Science teachers in Puerto Rico and Korea using my poems and songs. They're probably using my book and poems right now. Enjoy it. The "magic of rhyme" will make learning easier most of the time.

CONTENTS

Introduction 1

The Animal Cell. 5

The Animal Cell Activities. 16

The Paramecium 18

The Paramecium Cell Activities 24

All About Mitosis 28

Mitosis Activities 37

Deoxyribonucleic Acid (DNA) 44

DNA Activities 48

The Cell Olympiad 50

The Cell Olympiad Activities 66

The 10 Activities Of Life! 82

What Am I? Plant or Animal? 94

The Bean Plant! 106

The Life of A Pitcher Plant 109

The Teeth of Different Animals 116

The Teeth of Fish 121

Starfish 129

The Grasshopper 133

The Inchworm 142

The Ant 146

Food Tests 171

Classification Of Vertebrates 177

M & M's 184

INTRODUCTION

"Humpty Dumpty sat on a wall.
Humpty Dumpty had a great fall.
All the king's horses and all the king's men,
Couldn't put Humpty together again."

For most of you the preceding rhyme was very familiar. Most of you learned this rhyme at a very early age, even before you could read. Did you ever wonder why you were able to learn it so fast? Were the words associated so well that it made reading unnecessary? What did you learn from the poem? Probably the dangers of height and the dangers of being injured and maybe even an insight into the field of medicine. All this may have been captured by this small poem. If you read a story about the same incident, do you think that you would have arrived at the same conclusions? Would you have learned it as fast or remembered it to this day? I doubt it.

I believe that when words are associated in the "music" of rhyme, it is easier for the listener to understand and learn the meaning behind the poem. For example, if everyone were to read a page or two or even look at a chart illustrating the number of days in the months of the year, it would probably take some time to organize this in your mind and remember them. However, I remember the number of days in every month by reciting a poem which I memorized in grade school.

"Thirty days have September,
April, June and November.
All the rest have thirty-one,
Except the second month alone,
To which we twenty-eight assign,
Till leap year brings it twenty-nine."

**"The Magic of Rhyme-
Makes Learning Easier
Most of the Time"**

A quick memorization of this poem pinpoints the knowledge of the number of days in the months of the year.

In reading, you are only using the faculty of sight to observe the words you are reading. You must then put these words in some logical order within your mind to receive the important facts included in the reading. But in poetry, you are reinforced by the auditory nerves as well as by sight. These words are already expressed in a logical order. The important facts to be learned are there. The music of the rhyme appeals to the ear and registers easily in the mental faculty. If you doubt then, then perhaps you can explain to me why the lowest readers in my class, even those who know nothing about reading, are able to know the words to the top songs on the radio. Not only have they learned these words, but also the meanings behind them. Isn't this type of learning by rhyme more receptive to the listener than pages of reading?

This "magic" of rhyme was used in my seventh grade biology classes at Hubbard Junior High School in Plainfield. My poems were used to reinforce and introduce topics in the text and also to teach concepts of biology which are not covered sufficiently by the text.

At first, I wrote poems to make learning in my classroom fun and to break up the usual routine of lecturing and reading. But, after hearing my first poem, the students kept asking me to write others. From that day on, I recognized the importance of learning through rhyme. I wrote poems about almost every topic we discussed. My students were learning faster and were stimulated to read the text. Slow students were doing better work. Average students were doing above average work. The students became confident in reading the text since *the poems had arranged the topics in a logical and understandable order in their minds. More discussion and involvement took place.*

The students seemed to understand the concepts of biology faster since they were expressed in simple form. For example, for many students reading two or three pages about the grasshopper would become a difficult or uninteresting task, and to memorize its parts and functions would seem just as difficult.

To motivate an interest in the reading and the parts of the grasshopper, I used a poem as an introduction. The students turned to the picture of the grasshopper in their texts and we read the poem together. The students read two lines of the poem and found the parts described in the poem in the picture in their texts. For example, the first two lines read:

"Some grasshoppers are green, some appear red.
They have a thorax, abdomen and head."

After the students found these general parts, they went on to read:

"As small as they are, they really do well.
They have little antennae to feel and to smell."

The students looked for the antennae and underlined the purpose in the poem. The poem continued and the magical sounds of word association made learning the grasshopper, its parts and functions, an easy thing. *Learning became fun and learning became real.*

I also used poems to teach topics which were not fully covered by the textbook. The topic of mitosis presented such a problem. The text had pictures of the steps of mitosis but it did not fully explain what happened in mitosis or why it happened. The poem I wrote enabled me to teach the concept of mitosis without using a textbook. To help the students understand why mitosis took place I wrote:

"When a cell becomes too big and wide,
To live a good life, the cell must divide.
For it can't find all of the food that it needs.
And can't find enough oxygen. How can it breathe?"

After this I had to define Mitosis. The poem went on to read:

"My name is Mitosis. I perform very well.
I divide and I reproduce the cell.
I reproduce things in the nuclei,
And all of the protoplasm I will divide."

Then I used each additional stanza of the poem to describe individual phases of Mitosis. The students drew each phase on paper as they learned it from the poem. This method of learning was easier for them. They even filled in blank phases from the book and understood the name of the phase and what happened.

Since then I've used the magic of rhyme to teach students and provide workshops for my elementary teachers. We use hands-on science and music and rhyme to make learning about science fun. I hope you enjoy learning with this book. The magic of rhyme will make it easier and more fun to learn.

"Learning science requires concentration.
Use poems and songs to supply motivation.
They're a sauce for your learning to make reading fun.
Rhymes will be remembered forever by everyone."

**"The Magic of Rhyme –
Makes Learning Easier
Most of the Time"**

This book is dedicated to all of my students, year after year, and teachers, workshop after workshop, who have inspired me to write poems and songs to make their learning more fun and more memorable.

Thanks from Albert J. Musmanno Sr.

Use the blank pages for your own drawings, poems or notes.

Answers to many of the questions on the pages are in the back of the book. Try them first, then look to check. Be adventurous!
Have fun!

THE ANIMAL CELL

I am a cell an important part of you – and without me I don't know what you'd do.

Millions of me get together in you – to help do the things that you do.

What do I look like? Let me begin. I'm round or oval or sometimes quite thin.

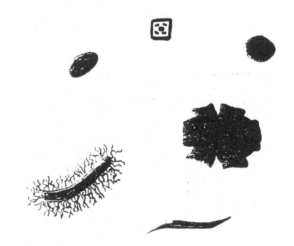

I am a cell, I am a cell – I'm swell. I help you make your body well- I am a cell

And the way I protect my body – you see- is by the membrane I have around me.

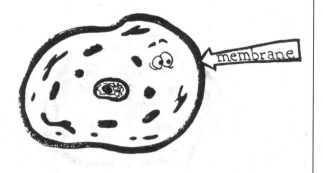

You have a brain made up of my cells. – And because of you – your muscles will swell.

I'm in your eyes, your ears and your feet. –And without me – your heart wouldn't beat.

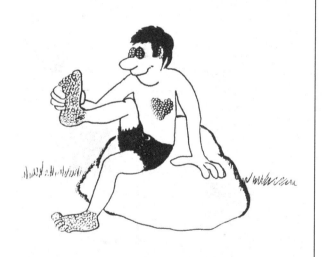

My most important part is my nucleus they say, The center of my activity – which contains DNA.

Not to mention its
membrane you know –
Which protects my insides-
which have chromosomes.

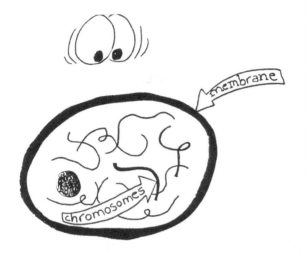

You have blood to live very nice. Well, my
blood is protoplasm – the substance of life

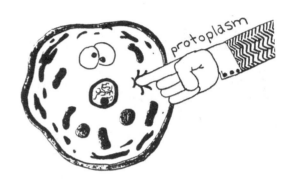

I have no lungs but I have a breathing station,
It's called mitochondrion-purpose respiration

And although I help you to eat –yes, you know,
I've got to eat through my food vacuole.'

And after I eat – my protein – I'll send –
through my enoplasmic reticulum

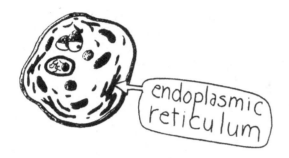

Well I'm just a cell. Quite small- don't you
know. and because of me you'll continue to
grow.

Well time is a wastin-
I must say goodbye.
It's just about time for me
to divide.

I am a cell. I am a cell, I'm swell. I help you
make you body well. I am a cell

For drawings, notes or poems!

THE ANIMAL CELL

I am a cell an important part of you,
And without me I don't know what you'd do.
Millions of me get together in you
To help you do the things that you do.

I am a cell. I am a cell. I'm swell.
I help you make your body well. I am a cell.   chorus

What do I look like? Let me begin.
I'm round or oval or sometimes quite thin.
And the way I protect my body you see
Is by the membrane I have around me.

I am a cell. I am a cell. I'm swell.
I help you make your body well. I am a cell.   chorus

You have a brain made up of my cells.
And because of me your muscles will swell.
I'm in your eyes your ears and your feet
And without me your heart wouldn't beat.

I am a cell. I am a cell. I'm swell.
I help you make your body well. I am a cell.   chorus

My most important part is my nucleus they say,
The center of my activity, which contains DNA.
Not to mention its membrane, you know,
Which protects my insides which have chromosomes.

I am a cell. I am a cell. I'm swell.
I help you make your body well. I am a cell.   chorus

You have blood to live very nice.
Well, my body is protoplasm, the substance of life.
I have no lungs but I have a breathing station.
It's called mitochondrion, purpose – respiration.

I am a cell. I am a cell. I'm swell.
I help you make your body well. I am a cell.   chorus

And although I help you to eat, yes you know,
I've got to eat through my food vacuole.
And after I eat, my protein I'll send
Through my endoplasmic reticulum.

I am a cell. I am a cell. I'm swell.
I help you make your body well. I am a cell.   chorus

Well, I'm just a cell, quite small, don't you know,
And because of me you'll continue to grow.
Well time is a'wastin', I must say goodbye.
It's just about time for me to divide.

I am a cell. I am a cell. I'm swell.
I help you make your body well. I am a cell.   chorus

You might want to look at the Animal Cell poem or song to help you fill in the functions of the cell parts listed below. Fill in what they do.

Cell membrane:_____

Nucleus:_____

Protoplasm:_____

Mitochondrion:_____

Food vacuole:_____

Endoplasmic reticulum:_____

Nuclear membrane:_____

Let's see how much you remember! Fill in the blanks from memory.

THE ANIMAL CELL

I am a cell an important part of you,
And without me I don't know what you'd do.
Millions of me get together in you
To help you do the things that you do.

I am a cell. I am a cell. I'm swell.
I help you make your body well. I am a cell.   chorus

What do I look like? Let me begin.
I'm round or oval or sometimes quite thin.
And the way I protect my body you see
Is by the _____ I have around me.

I am a cell. I am a cell. I'm swell.
I help you make your body well. I am a cell.   chorus

You have a brain made up of my cells.
And because of me your muscles will swell.
I'm in your eyes your ears and your feet
And without me your heart wouldn't beat.

I am a cell. I am a cell. I'm swell.
I help you make your body well. I am a cell.   chorus

My most important part is my _____ they say,
The center of my activity, which contains _____.
Not to mention its membrane, you know,
Which protects my insides which have _____.

I am a cell. I am a cell. I'm swell.
I help you make your body well. I am a cell.   chorus

You have blood to live very nice.
Well, my blood is _____, the substance of life.
I have no lung but I have a breathing station.
It's called mitochondrion, purpose - _____.

I am a cell. I am a cell. I'm swell.
I help you make your body well. I am a cell.   chorus

And although I help you to eat, yes you know,
I've got to eat through my _____.

13

And after I eat, my protein I'll send
Through my _____.

I am a cell. I am a cell. I'm swell.
I help you make your body well. I am a cell.   chorus
Well, I'm just a cell, quite small, don't you know,
And because of me you'll continue to grow.
Well time is a'wastin', I must say goodbye.
It's just about time for me to _____.

I am a cell. I am a cell. I'm swell.
I help you make your body well. I am a cell.   chorus

14

Draw your own animal cell and label its parts.

Write a poem about your cell.

Let's see how much you remember. Fill in the blanks.

THE ANIMAL CELL ACTIVITIES

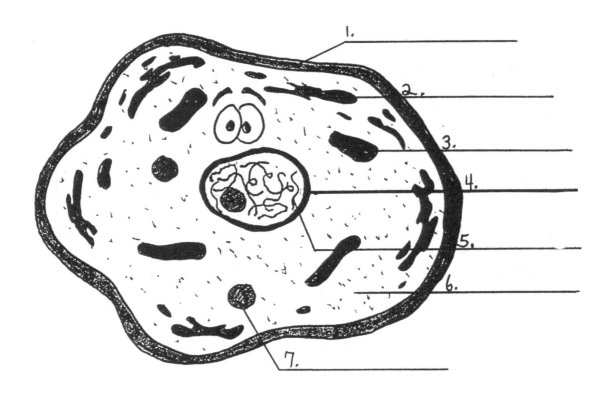

1. _____   5. _____

2. _____   6. _____

3. _____   7. _____

4. _____

Most plant cells have two things that an animal cell doesn't have. They are chloroplasts, which help them make food through photosynthesis, and a non-living cell wall around the membrane to protect the inside of the cell. Try drawing and labeling a plant cell.

Write a poem about your plant cell.

THE PARAMECIUM

A One-Celled Animal

THE PARAMECIUM
A One-Celled Animal

The Paramecium

My name is Paramecium. I'm only one cell. I'm known as an animal. I live very well.

Although I'm small, you can come and see me, I live in the puddles and ponds by your street

I don't eat fish, meat or sweets
I eat the bacteria that lives on
your street.
And I love tiny organisms, They
taste so crisp, I paralyze them
with my trichocysts

Then my food vacuole carries my
food all around. While enzymes
inside it break. my food down.

And of course I have
protoplasm,-every cell must-
And I;ve got a large and small
nucleus,

But, sexually, I'll reproduce ?? try

In conjugation, I'll exchange nuclei

And if I got too big and my body's too wide.
I'll reproduce asexually—I will divide

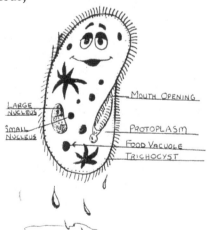

I'm not a girl or a boy you see.

So next time you go by a Puddle- you know—
Look down at me and just say hello

But don't look too long. I don't want to be rude.
I must move on and look for more food.

Draw your own paramecium. Label its parts.

Write a poem or story about your paramecium.

THE PARAMECIUM

My name is paramecium, I'm only one cell.
I'm known as an animal. I live very well.
Although I'm small, you can come and see me.
I live in the puddles and ponds by your street.

How do I eat? You might want to know.
Through my mouth opening or food vacuole.
I don't eat fish, meat or sweets.
I eat the bacteria that live on your street.

And I love tiny organisms, they taste so crisp.
I paralyze them with my trichocysts.
Then my food vacuole carries my food all around,
While the enzymes inside it break my food down.

And of course I have protoplasm, every cell must.
And I've got a large and small nucleus.
I'm not a girl or a boy you see.
I'm no special sex, I'm just me.

But sexually I'll reproduce if I try.
In conjugation I exchange nuclei.
And if I get too big and my body's too wide,
I'll reproduce asexually, I will divide.

So next time you go by a puddle you know,
Look down at me and just wave hello.
But don't look too long. I don't want to be rude.
I must move on and look for more food.

Use this page for notes, drawings or your poems or songs.

THE PARAMECIUM CELL ACTIVITIES

Let's see how much you remember. Fill in the blanks from memory.

My name is paramecium, I'm only one cell.
I'm known as an animal. I live very well.
Although I'm small, you can come and see me.
I live in the _____ and _____ by your street.

How do I eat? You might want to know.
Through my mouth opening or _____.
I don't eat fish, meat or sweets.
I eat the bacteria that live on your street.

And I love tiny organisms, they taste so crisp.
I paralyze them with my _____.
Then my _____ carries my food all around,
While the enzymes inside it break my food down.

And of course I have protoplasm, every cell must.
And I've got a large and small _____.
I'm not a girl or a boy you see.
I'm no special sex, I'm just me.

But sexually I'll reproduce if I try.
In conjugation I exchange nuclei.
And if I get too big and my body's too wide,
I'll reproduce asexually, I will _____.

So next time you go by a puddle you know,
Look down at me and just wave hello.
But don't look too long. I don't want to be rude.
I must move on and look for more food.

Try writing your own paramecium cartoon story.

Let's see how much you remember. Fill in the blanks from memory.

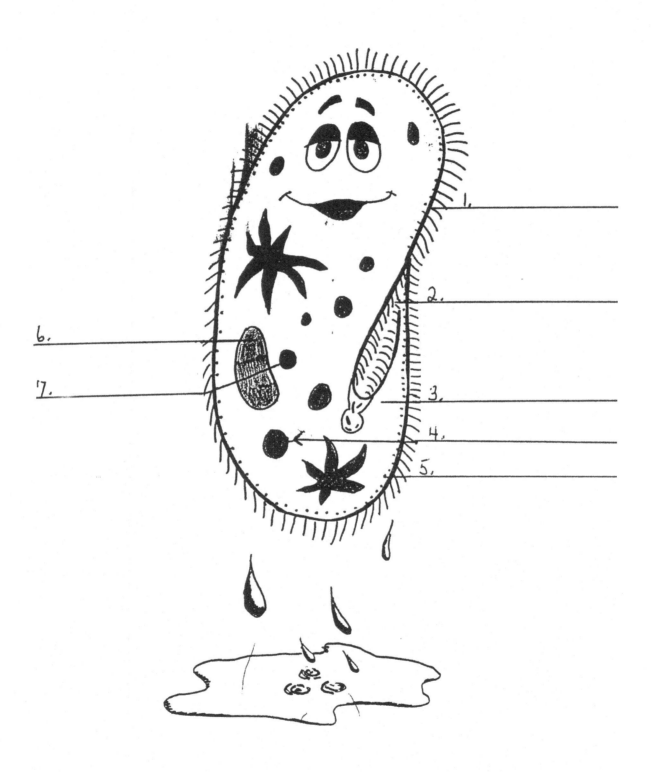

Use this page for notes, drawings or your poems or songs.

ALL ABOUT MITOSIS

MY NAME IS MITOSIS (See next page after reading)

When a cell becomes too big and too wide,
To live a good life, the cell must divide.
For it can't find all the food that it needs.
And can't find enough oxygen. How can it breathe?

So my name is Mitosis, I perform very well.
I divide and I reproduce the cell.
I reproduce things in the nuclei.
And all of the protoplasm, I will divide.

The first step of me you know very well.
In this step I'm just a normal cell.
This step is *interphase*, the beginning of much.
You might notice me by my nucleus.

Now I'm step two, *prophase* to you.
I guess you wonder Just what I'll do.
My chromatin shortens and thickens you see,
And forms the chromosomes in the nucleus of me.
Then my chromosomes duplicate. WOW, what a hit.
And each equal half is a chromatid.
My nucleolus is gone. What's going on here?
And my nuclear membrane just disappeared.

Now I'm in *metaphase*, look at my state.
Chromosomes on the equatorial plate.
And each little chromosome each has a goal,
To go to the north or the south spindle pole.
They travel on a fiber, so they won't dwindle.
The name of it is the mitotic spindle.
And the second my chromosomes start towards the poles,
Step four, *anaphase*, has started to roll.

In *anaphase*, the chromosomes will go
Towards the north or south spindle pole.
At the end of the journey in the poles they will lie,
And I will be ready to change to step five.

Step five is here. I'm *telephase*, I'm swell.
I get together the parts of the cell.
My chromosomes will again get long and thin,
And change right back into chromatin.
My nucleolus has come back you see.
And my nuclear membrane forms around me.

29

My protoplasm divided, nucleus reproduced.
Review all the steps Mitosis has used.

For each one of these cells is equal you see.
I have equal chromosomes in each half of me.
And don't think my chromosomes were just torn apart.
They reproduced from the ones at the start.
Remember my new cells, remember them well.
Each one is called a new *daughter cell*.
Now I must run. No time to waste.
Back to step one. I'm just interphase

INTERPHASE

PROPHASE

METAPHASE

ANAPHASE

TELOPHASE

DAUGHTER CELLS

INTERPHASE

Use this page for notes, drawings or your poems or songs.

When a cell becomes too big and too wide,
To live a good life, the cell must divide.
For it can't find all the food that it needs.
And can't find enough oxygen. How can it breathe?

So my name is Mitosis, I perform very well.
I divide and I reproduce the cell.
I reproduce things in the nuclei.
And all of the protoplasm, I will divide.

DEFINITION OF MITOSIS

The division of the protoplasm and parts of the cell, and the reproduction of the present nucleus and its parts.

The first step of me, you know very well. In this step I;m just a normal cell. This step is interphrase- the beginning of much,

You might notice me by my nucleus,

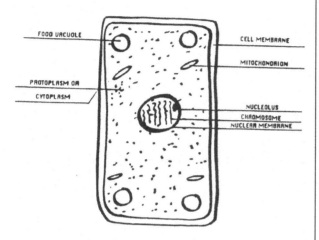

THINGS THAT HAPPENED

1. Thinning of the chromosomes

Now I'm step two, Prophase to you, I guess you wonder just what I'll do.My chromatin shortens and thickens you see.
And forms the chromosomes in the nucleus of me. Then my chromosomes duplicate,,-Wow, what a hit.
And each equal half is a chromatid. My nucleolus is gone. What's going on here?

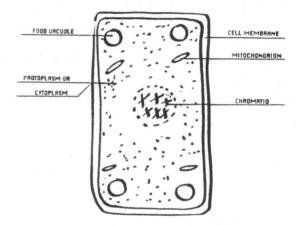

And my nuclear membrane just disappeared.
THINGS THAT HAPPENED
1. Chromatin shortens, thickens
2. Chromosomes duplicate
3. Nucleolus disappears
4. Nuclear membrane disappears

Now I'm in Metaphase=Look at my state – Chromosomes on the equatorial plate, And each little chromosome, each has a goal, To go to the north or the south spindle pole. They travel on a fiber so they won't dwindle. The name of it is the mitotic spindle.

And the second my chromosomes start towards the poles- Step four, Anaphase has started to roll.

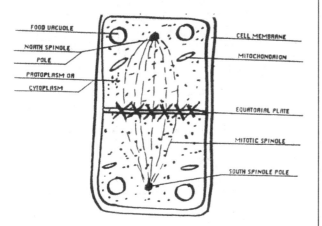

THINGS THAT HAPPENED
1. Equatorial plate forms in the middle
2. North & South spindle poles form

In Anaphase the chromosomes will go-towards the north or south spindle pole,

At the end of their journey, in the poles they will lie, And I wil be ready to change to step five.

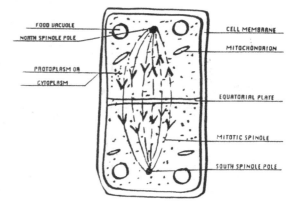

THINGS THAT HAPPENED
1. Chromosomes move toward north and south spindle pole.

Step five is here, I'm telophase, I'm swell, I get together the parts of the cell My chromosomes will again get along and thin – and change right back into chromatin.
My Nucleolus has come back you see – and my Nuclear membrane forms around me.

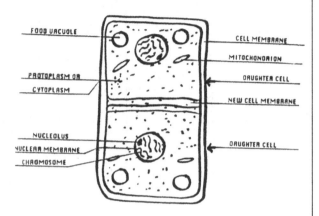

My protoplasm divided. Nucleus reproduced- review all the steps that Mitosis has used.

THINGS THAT HAPPENED
1. Chromosomes will again get long and thin and change right back into chromatin
2. Nucleolus comes back
3. Nuclear membrane- reforms
4. Protoplasm & parts divided
5. Nucleus reproduced in both cells

.For each one of these cells are equal you see. I have equal chromosomes in each half of me. And don't think my chromosomes were just torn apart. They reproduced from the ones at the start.
Remember my new cells, remember them well. Each one is called a new daughter cell.

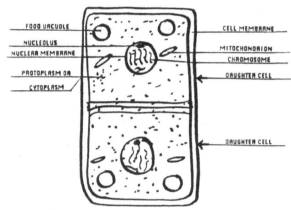

Now I must run – no time to waste.
Back to step one – I'm just interphase.

THINGS THAT HAPPENED
1. Equal chromosomes in each cell
2. Each cell is called a new daughter cell

MITOSIS ACTIVITIES

DRAW *INTERPHASE* AND FILL IN "THINGS THAT HAPPENED".

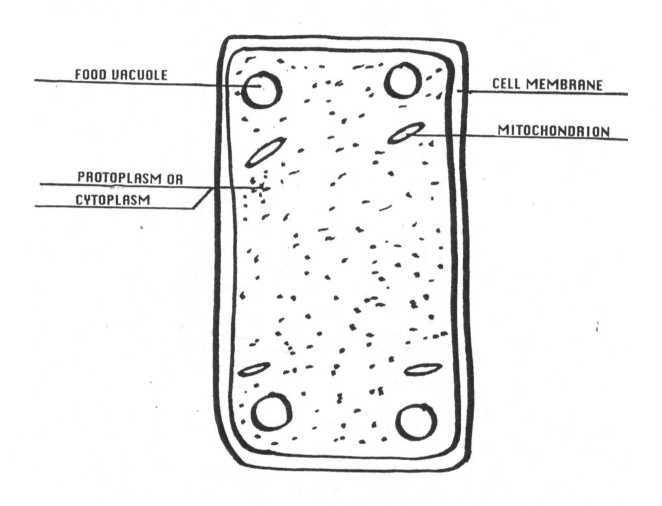

THINGS THAT HAPPENED

1. _____

DRAW *PROPHASE* AND FILL IN "THINGS THAT HAPPENED".

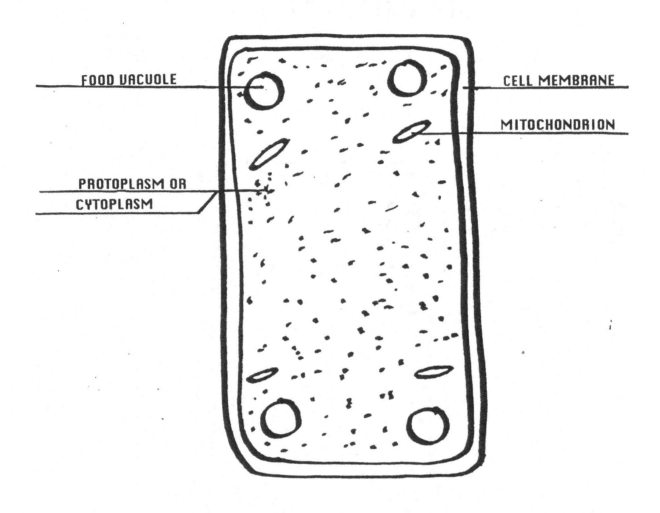

THINGS THAT HAPPENED

1.

2.

3.

4.

DRAW *METAPHASE* AND FILL IN "THINGS THAT HAPPENED".

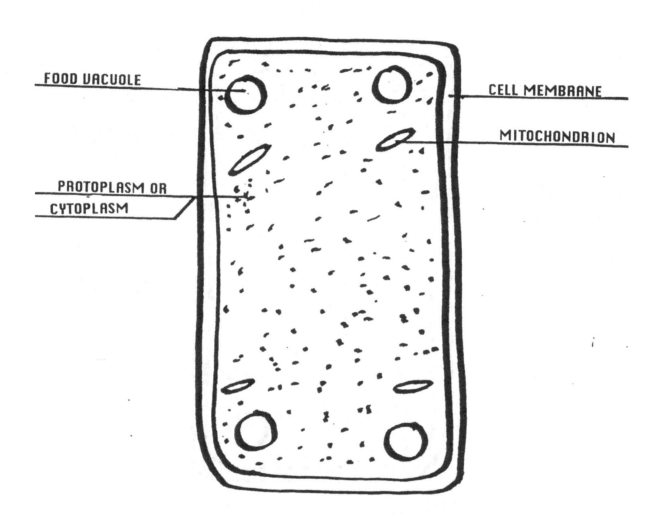

THINGS THAT HAPPENED

1. _____

_____

2. _____

_____

_____

DRAW *ANAPHASE* AND FILL "THINGS THAT HAPPENED".

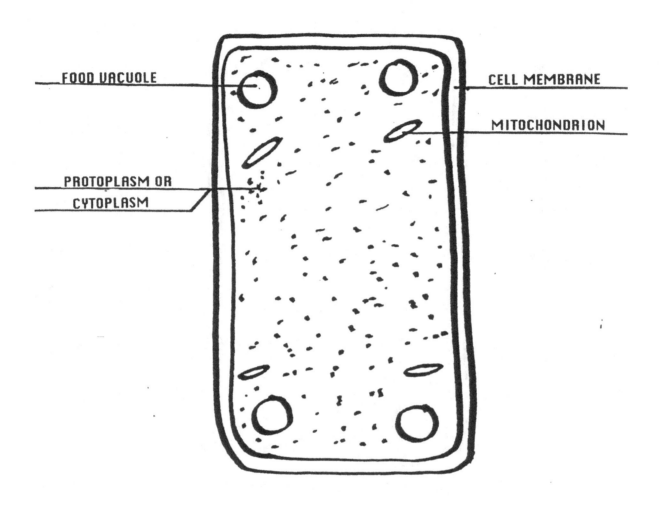

THINGS THAT HAPPENED

1.

DRAW *TELOPHASE* AND FILL IN "THINGS THAT HAPPENED".

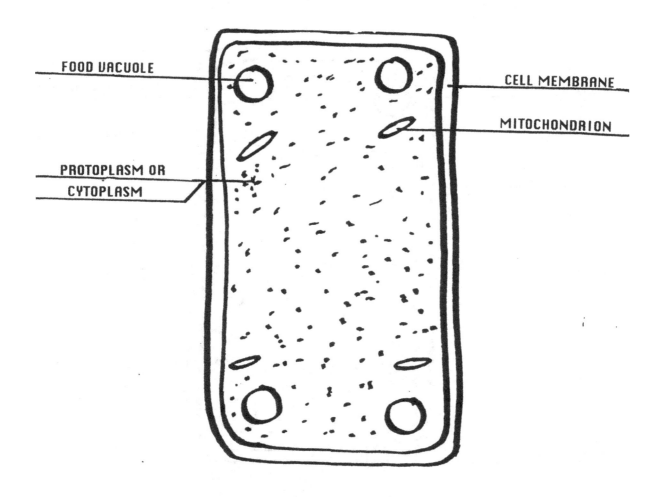

THINGS THAT HAPPENED

1.

2.

3.

4.

5.

DRAW THE *DAUGHTER CELLS* AND FILL IN "THINGS THAT HAPPENED".

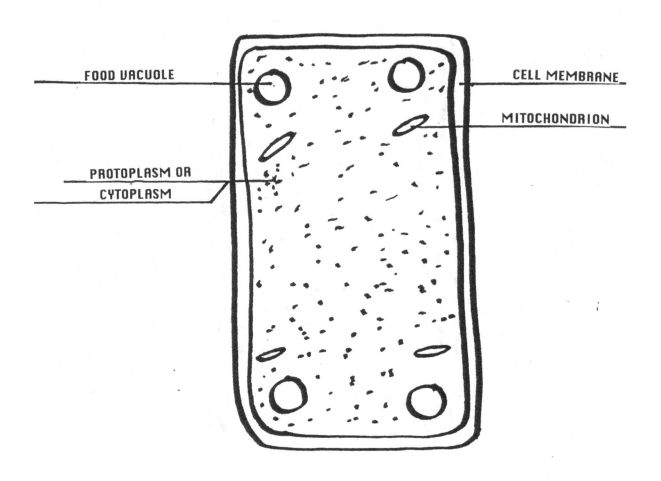

THINGS THAT HAPPENED

1. _____

_____

2. _____

_____

WHAT IS THE DEFINITION OF MITOSIS?

_____

_____

_____

_____

_____

WHAT ARE THE PHASES OF MITOSIS?

_____

_____

_____

_____

_____

DEOXYRIBONUCLEIC ACID (DNA)

Our names are adenine and thymine.
We're buddies of guanine and cytosine.
We're found together, but we're not the same.
We're chemically different. We form DNA.

We're found in the chromosomes of your cells.
We guide heredity and work really well.
The side of the ladder is the strongest to date,
Where sugar and phosphate bonds alternate.

At the rungs sugar forms a chemical bond,
And only on sugar will we latch on.
Cytosine with guanine, adenine and thymine.
In this type of pairing is the way we are seen.

So look at the world and how parents today,
Have children who look like them in some little way.
In animals and plants, it's just the same way.
On where would life be without DNA.

In DNA, adenine is always found with _____.

Guanine is always found with _____

_____

Draw DNA as a ladder. Use the picture on the following page to help you. Try to label its parts. You can even go back to read the poem to help you.

_____

D.N.A.

Our names are Adenine and
Thymine.
We're buddies of Guanine
and Cytosine.
We're found together but
we're not the same.
We're chemically different,
We form DNA.

D.N.A.

Our names are Adenine and thymine. We're buddies of Guanine and Cytosine.

We're found together but we're not the same. We're chemically different. We form DNA.

We're found in the chromosomes of your cell. We guide heredity and work really well.

The side of the ladder is the strongest to date. Where sugar and phosphate bonds alternate

At the rungs, sugar forms a chemical bond. And only on sugar —will we latch on.

Cytosine and Guanine, Adenine with thymine. In this type of pairing is the way we are seen.

So look at the world and how parents today, Have children who look like them in some little way.
In animals and plants. It's just the same way.
Oh, where would life be without DNA

Can you make a DNA model with different shapes of macaroni (ziti, rigatoni etc.)

You can even use toothpicks and different colors of spice candies.

Plan your model below!
Have Fun!

DNA ACTIVITIES

Let's see how much you remember. Fill in the blanks from memory.

Our names are adenine and _____.
We're buddies of guanine and _____.
We're found together, but we're not the same.
We're chemically different. We form DNA.

We're found in the chromosomes of your cells.
We guide heredity and work really well.
The side of the ladder is the strongest to date,
Where sugar and _____ bonds alternate.

At the rungs sugar forms a chemical bond,
And only on sugar will we latch on.
Cytosine with guanine, _____ and thymine.
In this type of pairing is the way we are seen.

So look at the world and how parents today,
Have children who look like them in some little way.
In animals and plants, it's just the same way.
Oh where would life be without _____.

Find the partner. Fill in the other side of the run of the ladder of life – DNA. Use guanine, cytosine, adenine and thymine for fill-ins. Go back to the poem if you need help.

guanine	_____
cytosine	_____
thymine	_____
adenine	_____
thymine	_____
guanine	_____

THE CELL OLYMPIAD

One large pond was divided into four different areas.

In the first area, near the road, there was a part which everyone in the pond knew as *Flagellata*. This part of the pond was muddy and, very deep. In this section lived the flagellates, cells with long whip-like strands called flagella. These flagellates were called Euglenas.

Nobody ever went over to visit them because of the dirty water around them. However, if you got close enough to their area, you could hear the long strands of flagella whipping back and forth and cracking like bullwhips as the Euglenas moved through the water. The Euglenas never swam anywhere else in the pond because they felt no other place in the pond was deep enough to allow their long strands of flagella to whip back and forth.

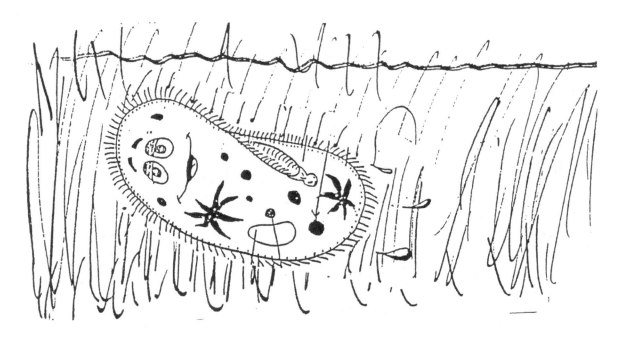

Towards the middle of the pond there was a very shallow section full of weeds. This part of the pond was called *Ciliata* because the Paramecium which lived there had hundreds of little cilia around their bodies. They were very touch and could throw little spears or needles called *trichocysts* from their bodies at anyone who tried to push them around.

They spent their days hunting bacteria which were around the weeds, and they wouldn't allow anyone to come into their section because they were afraid the others would come and eat their bacteria. They were very greedy, thus no one in the pond liked them and no one visited them because they were afraid of being shot by their trichocysts.

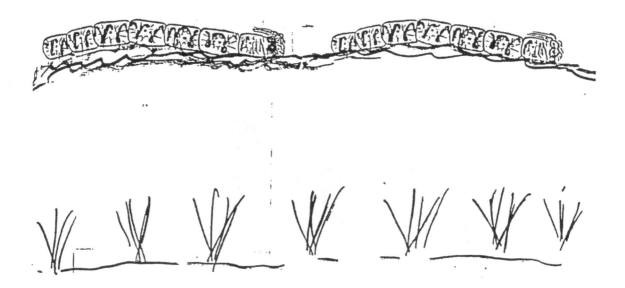

And then there was another part of the pond which was covered with trees that had fallen years ago. Green scum called *Spirogyra* lived all over the top of the water. They didn't bother anyone. They just floated around the pond and minded their own business, They didn't need anyone because they were green plant cells and could make their own food. They didn't have to go hunting for it.

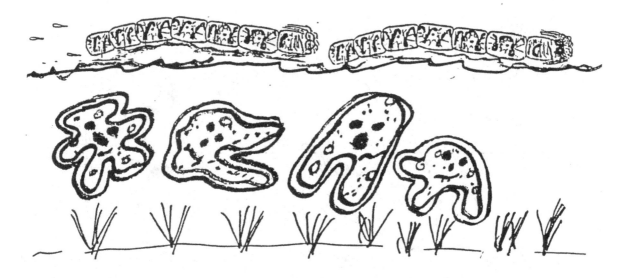

Near the bottom of the Spirogyra was the land of *Sarcodina*. This was the area where the *Amoebas* lived. They would blob around throwing their pseudopods and protoplasm around all day. They could move in any direction just by throwing the cytoplasm (protoplasm) in their bodies that way. The Spirogyra enjoyed watching them because they looked so acrobatic.

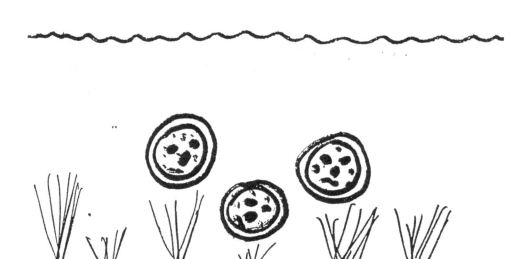

There were also some cells in the area of *Sporozoa*. They were most feared even though they couldn't move at all. All of these cells were spores and gave all types of diseases to the humans who walked by the pond. The most notorious of these cells was *Plasmodium Vivax*. It would give the disease called malaria.

Anyway, one day they had a community meeting of all the different parts of the pond. The president of each area came and they began to plan a *Cell Olympics* in the pond. The winner would be able to choose any new parts of the pond to live in without the worry of fighting and wars.

They had learned their lesson the hard way. Years ago, a war over areas almost wiped out the entire pone. After the war, the whole pond smelled of the dead cells, and there was fear of pollution and death for the following year.

Each area was to decide on an event for all four areas to compete in, but Plasmodium Vivax said his area would referee since cells in his area had no way of moving. Then the area of Spirogyra was ruled out of competition because they were plant cells. Sally Spirogyra protested because she believed the Euglenas from the area of Flagellata were also plants.

Eddie Euglena stood up and said, "We only have cell membranes and have no cell walls like plants." Sally Spirogyra screamed, "Well, what about your chloroplasts? You make your own food." A heated debate followed. They all put their nucleuses together and agreed on admitting Euglenas in the Olympics since they did have characteristics of an animal cell.

Sally screamed, I hope your flagella gets tied in knots and your chloroplasts turn red." Then she floated away.

Then Priscilla paramecium said that her area would challenge the Amoebas and Euglenas in the 100 inch dash. Albert Amoeba said Sarcodina would challenge in the hurdles, and Eddie Euglena said Flagellata challenged all in the broad jump.

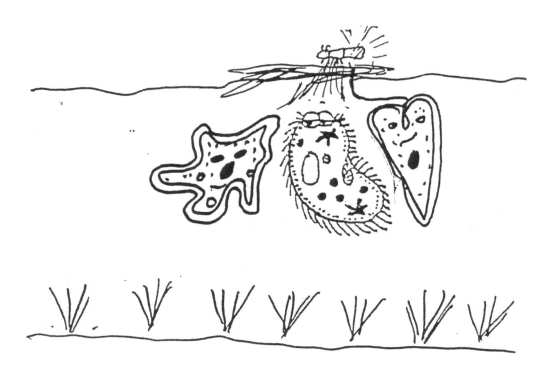

The day of the Olympics came and representative cells from all the parts of the pond sent hundreds of cells together, and they carried a firefly to the top of the twig in the area of the Olympiad.

All the cells in the pond watched as the athletes from Sarcodina (Amoebas), Flagellata (Euglenas) and Ciliata (Paramecium) paraded by for the opening ceremonies. The first event, the 100 inch dash, was about to begin.

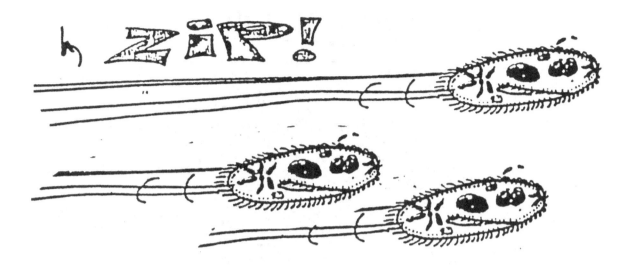

All the Paramecium won the 100 inch dash because of their many cilia which moved them like speed boats. The closest competition were the Euglenas who were 50 inches behind them because they only had one flagella to whip back and forth. This gave the Paramecium 5 points for first, 3 points for second and 1 point for third; 9 points all together.

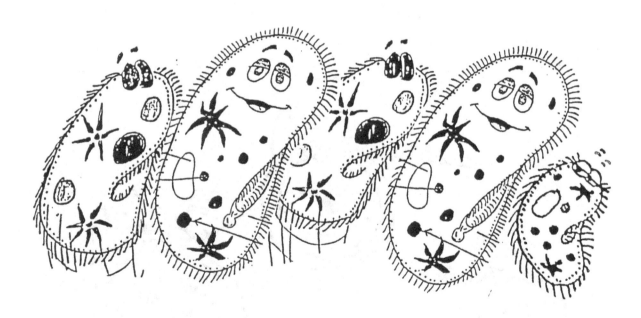

The crowd from Ciliata went wild, crashing their membranes together in thunderous applause. The applause was silenced by the start of the hurdles, the next event.

The Amoebas all won in the hurdles because they were able to move their protoplasm around each hurdle and didn't have to worry about jumping like the Euglenas and Paramecium. Now they also had 9 points, with the last event, the broad jump, about to start.

The crowd of cells were tense as they watched the last event. The Plasmodiums refereed carefully because they were afraid the cells would riot if they made a mistake.

Eddie Euglena started his approach. He put his flagella on the ground and pushed his cell way up into the air. A new cell record was scored. He jumped 23 centimeters. Earl and Eugene Euglena scored second and third with good jumps, and the Amoebas and Paramecium couldn't get high enough to jump.

The Olympics ended up in a tie, but in the crowd the Amoebas, Paramecium, Euglenas, Sporozoans and Spirogyra started talking and became friends. They agreed to have no set areas, but to live in the pond all together.

ANSWER THESE QUESTIONS ABOUT THE STORY

1. What are Flagellates?_____

2. What were the Flagellates called? _____

3. Who lived in Ciliata? _____

4. What did the Paramecium have around their bodies? _____

5. What are Spirogyra? _____

6. Who lived in Sarcodina? _____

   Draw what you think they looked like.

7. Who lived in Sporozoa? _____

   Draw what you think they looked like.

8. Why did the Paramecium win the 100 inch dash? _____

   _____

9. Why did the Amoebas win the hurdles? _____

   _____

10. Who won the broad jump? _____

    Why? _____

    _____

See if you can remember what the characters in the story looked like. Draw them above their names.

Priscilla Paramecium   *Eddie Euglena*

Plasmodium Vivax   *Al Amoeba*

Sally Spirogyra

Use this page for notes, drawings or your poems or songs.

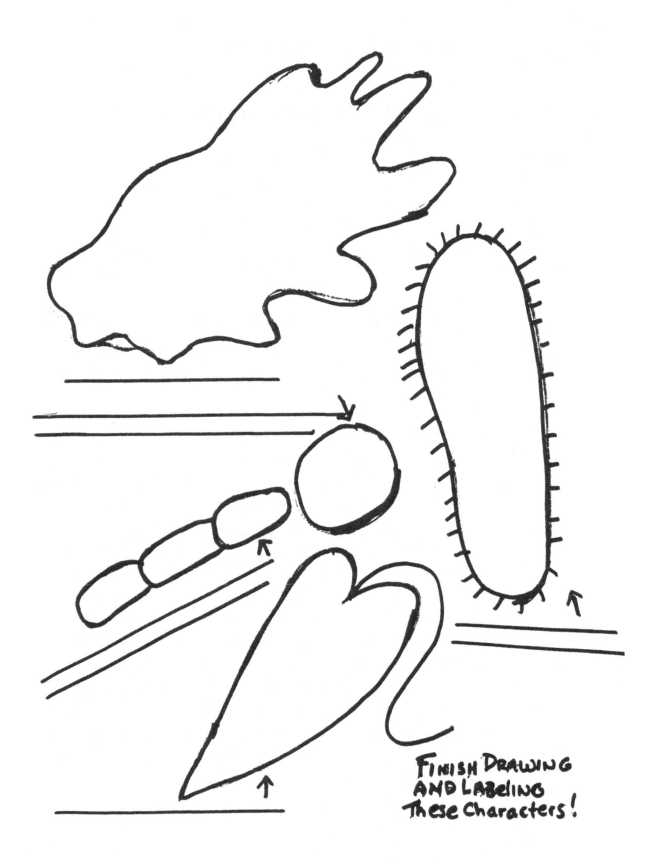

FINISH DRAWING
AND LABELING
These Characters!

Try to draw in the cartoons for *The Cell Olympiad* yourself. Here's the story. You draw the characters your way.

THE CELL OLYMPIAD ACTIVITIES

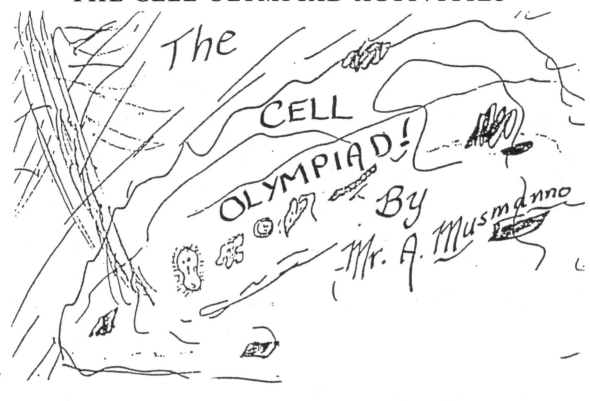

One large pond was divided into four different areas.

In the first area, near the road, there as a part which everyone in the pond knew as *Flagellata*. This part of the pond was muddy and very, very deep. In this section lived the flagellates, cells with long whip-like strands called flagella. These flagellates were called Euglenas.

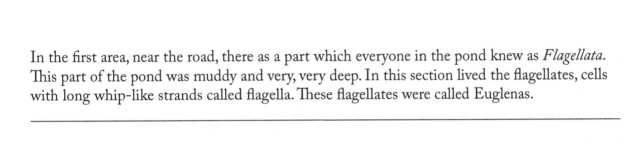

Nobody ever went over to visit them because of the dirty water around them. However, if you got close enough to their area, you could hear the long strands of flagella whipping back and forth and cracking like bullwhips as the Euglenas moved through the water. The Euglenas never swam anywhere else in the pond because they felt no other place in the pond was deep enough to allow their long strands of flagella to whip back and forth.

Toward the middle of the pond there was a very shallow section full of weeds. This part of the pond was called *Ciliata* because the Paramecium which lived there had hundreds of little cilia around their bodies. They were very tough and could throw little spears or needles called *trichocysts* from their bodies at anyone who tried to push them around.

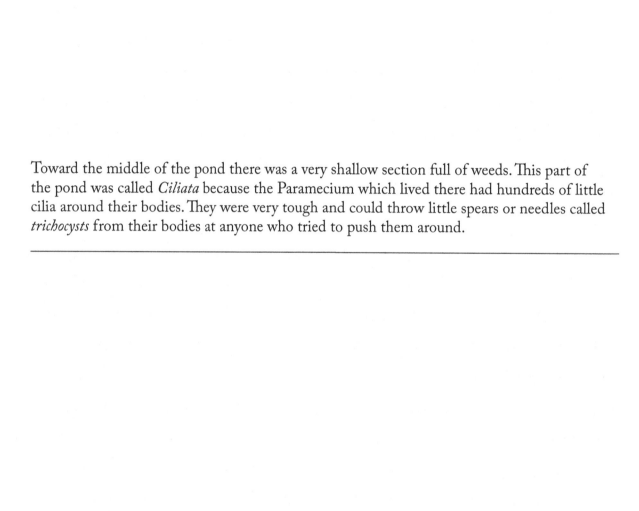

They spent their days hunting bacteria which were around the weeds, and they wouldn't allow anyone to come into their section because they were afraid the others would come and eat their bacteria. They were very greedy, thus no one in the pond liked them and no one visited them because they were afraid of being shot by their trichocysts.

And then there was another part of the pond which was covered with trees that had fallen years ago. Green scum called *Spirogyra* lived all over the top of the water. They didn't bother anyone. They just floated around the pond and minded their own business, They didn't need anyone because they were green plant cells and could make their own food. They didn't have to go hunting for it.

Near the bottom of the Spirigyra was the land of *Sarcodina*. This was the area where the *Amoebas* lived. They would blob around throwing their pseudopods and protoplasm around all day. They could move in any direction just by throwing the cytoplasm (protoplasm) in their bodies that way. The Spirogyra enjoyed watching them because they looked so acrobatic.

There were also come cells in the area of *Sporozoa*. They were most feared even though they couldn't move at all. All of these cells were spores and gave all types of diseases to the humans who walked by the pond. The most notorious of these cells wee *Plasmodium Vivax*. It would give the disease called malaria.

Anyway, one day they had a community meeting of all the different parts of the pond. The president of each area came and they began to plan a *Cell Olympics* in the pond. The winner would be able to choose any new parts of the pond to live in without the worry of fighting and wars.

They had learned their lesson the hard way. Years ago, a war over areas almost wiped out the entire pond. After the war, the whole pond smelled of the dead cells, and there was fear of pollution and death for the year following.

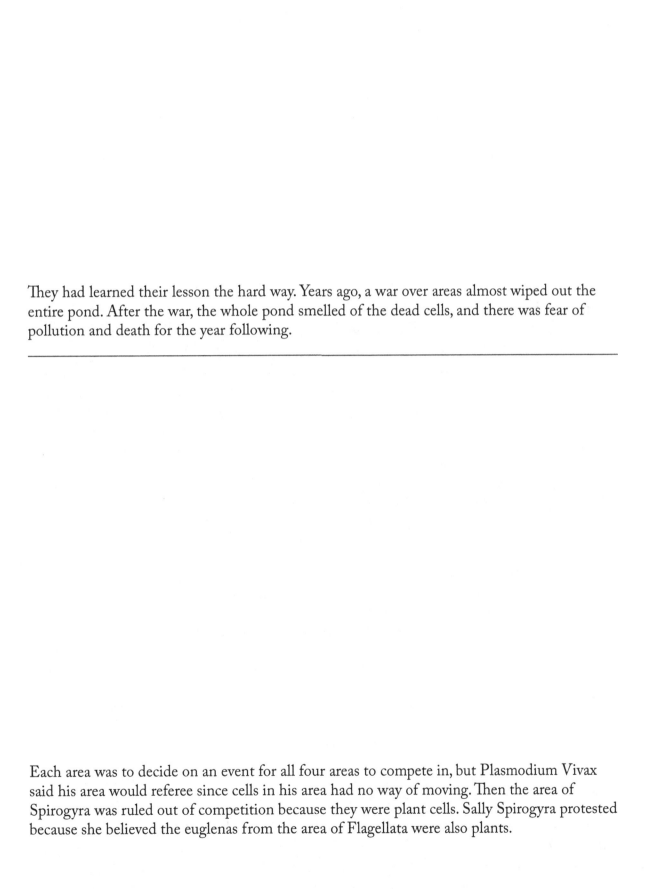

Each area was to decide on an event for all four areas to compete in, but Plasmodium Vivax said his area would referee since cells in his area had no way of moving. Then the area of Spirogyra was ruled out of competition because they were plant cells. Sally Spirogyra protested because she believed the euglenas from the area of Flagellata were also plants.

Eddie Euglena stood up and said, "We only have cell membranes and have no cell walls like plants." Sally Spirogyra screamed, "Well, what about your chloroplasts? You make your own food." A heated debate followed. They all put their nucleuses together and agreed on admitting Euglenas in the Olympics since they did have characteristics of an animal cell.

Sally screamed, I hope your flagella gets tied in knots and your chloroplasts turn red." Then she floated away.

Then Priscilla Paramecium said that her area would challenge the Amoebas and Euglenas in the 100 inch dash. Albert Amoeba said Sarcodina would challenge in the hurdles, and Eddie Euglena and Flagellata challenged all in the broad jump.

The day of the Olympics came and representative cells from all the parts of the pond sent hundreds of cells together, and they carried a firefly to the top of the twig in the area of the Olympiad.

All the cells in the pond watched as the athletes from Sarcodina (Amoebas), Flagellata (Euglenas) and Ciliata (Paramecium) paraded by for the opening ceremonies. The first event, the 100 inch dash, was about to begin.

All the Paramecium won the 100 inch dash because of their many cilia which moved them like speed boats. The closest competition were the Eugienas who were 50 inches behind them because they only had one flagella to whip back and forth. This gave the Paramecium 5 points for first, 3 points for second and 1 point for third; 9 points all together.

The crowd from Ciliata went wild, crashing their membranes together in thunderous applause. The applause was silenced by the start of the hurdles, the next event.

The Amoebas all won in the hurdles because they were able to move their protoplasm around each hurdle and didn't have to worry about jumping like the Euglenas and Paramecium. Now they also had 9 points, with the last event, the broad jump, about to start.

The crowd of cells was tense as they watched the last event. The Plasmodiums refereed carefully because they were afraid the cells would riot if they made a mistake.

Eddie Euglena started his approach. He put his flagella on the ground and pushed his cell way up into the air. A new cell record was scored. He jumped 23 centimeters. Earl and Eugene Euglena scored second and third with good jumps, and the Amoebas and Paramecium couldn't get high enough to jump.

The Olympics ended up in a lie, but in the crowd the Amoebas, Paramecium, Euglenas, Sporozoans and Spirogyra started talking and became friends. They agreed to have no set areas, but to live in the pond all together.

Get carpet foam and make your characters.

Cut carpet foam or styrofoam shapes like these.

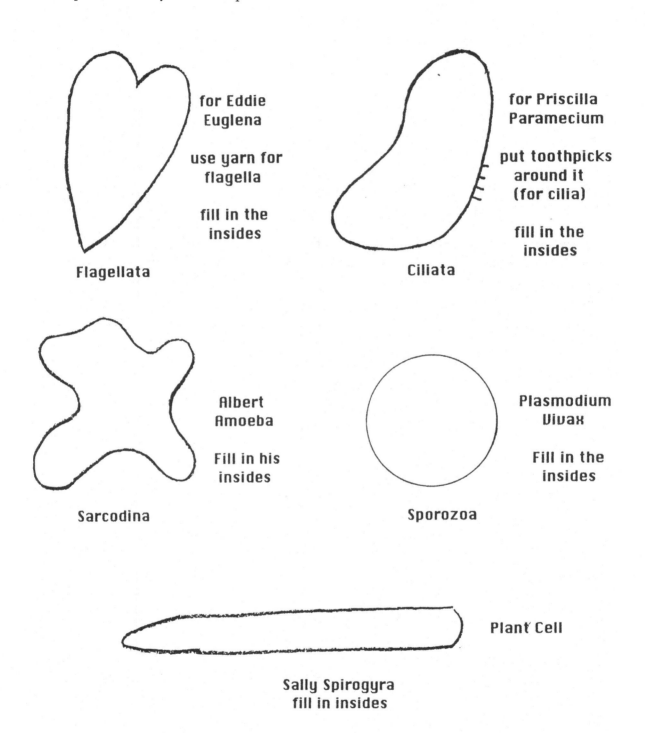

for Eddie
Euglena

use yarn for
flagella

fill in the
insides

Flagellata

for Priscilla
Paramecium

put toothpicks
around it
(for cilia)

fill in the
insides

Ciliata

Albert
Amoeba

Fill in his
insides

Sarcodina

Plasmodium
Vivax

Fill in the
insides

Sporozoa

Plant Cell

**Sally Spirogyra
fill in insides**

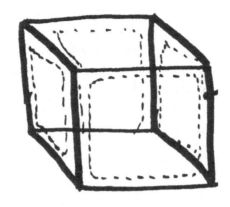

Label this cell membrane in animal
cells or cell wall and cell membrane in
plant cells.

Get a box. Cut out its sides. Hang the parts of the cell in it with thread or string. Label the
parts. You have a 3-dimensional cell made. (You'll need more parts for the plant cell)

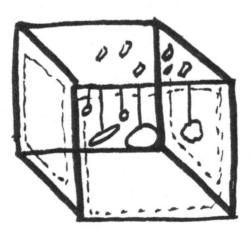

Tie or tape string on top.

Do this page first!!

Look them up in the
Dictionary – write the
Meaning by the
Activity of Life

What do these 10 life functions mean? Look them up in your dictionary. The definitions will help you fill in the poem about The Life of a Frog.

1. Food getting - _____

   _____

2. Reproduction - _____

   _____

3. Motion - _____

   _____

4. Sensitivity - _____

   _____

5. Excretion - _____

   _____

6. Respiration - _____

   _____

7. Assimilation - _____

   _____

8. Absorption - _____

   _____

9. Digestion - _____

   _____

10. Secretion - _____

   _____

How's your memory? Write the 10 activities of life below. If you have trouble, go back to page 80 or in the back on pages 188-189

THE 10 ACTIVITIES OF LIFE!

All living things perform
10 basic Activities which
we call LIFE
FUNCTIONS,
These 10 for animals are –
FOOD GETTING,
REPRODUCTION,
MOTION, SENSITIVITY,
EXCRETION,
RESPIRATION,
ASSIMILATION.
ABSORPTION
DIGESTION AND,
SECRETION.

The following poem will
refer to all 10 of these life
functions.

Write in the name of the life function at the end of the phrase – in the parenthesees,
THE LIFE OF A FROG

A frog in a pond might jump to a rock,
(_____)

It might eat an insect at one of its stops,
(_____)

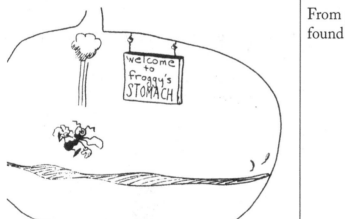

The food is taken to its stomach and then broken down (_____)

From glands in the stomach =these fluids are found (_____)

Then the nutrients are taken up by the blood.
(_____)

Food becomes living matter, as it should.

This will do the body well. It's used for growth or repair of the cell.
(_____)

Powerful lungs take in the oxygen that it needs,
(_____)

Waste products pass through the kidneys, from where they will leave.
(_____)

A frog might hear the call of its mate,

(_____)

And in the spring of the year, a female lays eggs,

(_____)

How's your memory? Write the 10 activities of life below. If you have trouble, go back to page 80 or 188 to 189.

After you write the
Activity of Life—Write
The definition of the
Activity.

Use this page for your notes or your own poems or songs or drawings about science.

All living things perform 10 basic activities which we call *life functions*. These 10 for animals are: *food getting, reproduction, motion, sensitivity, excretion, respiration, assimilation, absorption, digestion and secretion.*

The following poem will refer to all 10 of these life functions. Write in the name of the life function at the end of the phrase in the parentheses.

THE LIFE OF A FROG

A frog in a pond might jump to a rock. (_____)

It might eat an insect at one of its stops. (_____)

Food is taken to its stomach, then broken down. (_____)

From glands in the stomach, these fluids are found. (_____)

Then the nutrients are taken up by the blood. (_____)

Food becomes living matter, as it should. (_____)
This will do the body well.
It's used for growth or repair of the cell.

Powerful lungs take in the oxygen it needs. (_____)

Waste products pass through the kidneys, (_____)
     from where they will leave.

A frog might hear the call of its mate. (_____)

And in the spring of the year the female lays eggs. (_____)

Write a poem about the 10 activities of life. Use another animal, other than a frog, in your poem. How does it do the 10 activities of life? Plan this below.

HAVE YOU SEEN ME BEFORE?

WHAT AM I?

My body is green and I live in a strand.
I grow in the water. I don't grow on land.
I'm a cell of a plant, if that gives you a clue.
If you live by a pond, I live by you.

You might ask me how do I move?
Well I just float around and make my own food.
How do I make food? Take a wild guess,
The process is called photosynthesis.

I have a cell wall and cell membrane on me.
Without that protection, where would I be?
And my chloroplasts wind all around in my cell.
And the pyrenoids inside it make me look swell.

I've told you so much, what more can I say?
Well I reproduce in two different ways.
Asexually – mitosis, when my cell appears split.
Sexually – conjugation, have you guessed me yet?

If you haven't guess, I guess I have won.
People that don't know me call me green scum.
But people who know me won't call me the same.
They call me *spirogyra*, that's my real name.

Use this page for notes, drawings or your poems or songs.

Let's see how much you remember. Fill in the blanks from memory.

HAVE YOU SEEN ME BEFORE?

WHAT AM I?

My body is green and I live in a strand.
I grow in the water. I don't grow on _____.
I'm a cell of a plant, if that gives you a clue.
If you live by a pond, I live by you.

You might ask me how do I move?
Well I just float around and make my own _____.
How do I make food? Take a wild guess.
The process is called _____.

I have a cell wall and cell _____ on me.
Without that protection, where would I be?
And my _____ wind all around in my cell.
And the pyrenoids inside it make me look swell.

I've told you so much, what more can I say?
Well I reproduce in two different ways.
Asexually - _____, when my cell appears split.
Sexually – conjugation, have you guess me yet?

If you haven't guessed, I guess I have won.
People that don't know me call me green scum.
But people who know me won't call me the same.
They call me *spirogyra*, that's my real name.

Draw the spirogyra on page 114. Write your own poem or story about it.

WHAT AM I? PLANT OR ANIMAL?

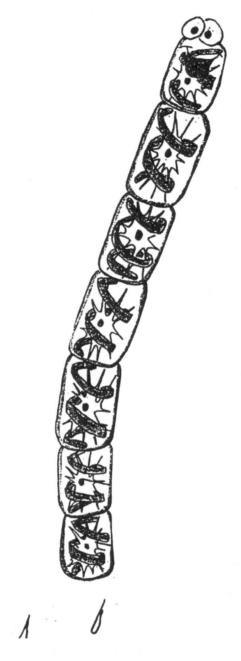

Have You Seen Me Before?

What Am I?   Plant or Animal?

Have
You Seen
Me
Before?

Is this a plant or an animal?
What Am I?

My body is green and I live in
a strand. I grow in the water. I
don't grow on land.
I'm a cell of a plant if that gives
you clue. If you live by a long. I
live by you.
You might ask me – How do I
move? Well I just float around
and make my own food.
How do I make food?
Take a wild guess. The
Process is called
Photosynthesis.
I have a cell wall and cell membrane on me.
Without that protection, where would I be?

And my chromosomes wind all around in my
cell. And the pyrenoids inside me make me
look swell.

I've told you so much. What more can I say?
Well I reproduce in two different ways.

Asexually – Mitosis- when my cell appears
split. Sexually- conjugation-Have you guessed
me yet?

If you haven't guessed yet I guess I've won.
People that don't know me call me green scum.

But people who – know me
Won't call me the same. They'll
Call me SPIROGYRA. That's
My real name.

Spirogyra is green algae. Color it green. Draw and color red algae, blue-green algae and yellow algae below.

What am I?

Open your refrigerator. What do you see? If it's moist or not cold enough, you may see me.
I live on your ham, your bread or your sweets, I live on anything that you like to eat.

As long as it's moist I'll continue to thrive, You might get rid of me by making me dry.
I can be harmful or beneficial to you. I am a mold,. I can't make my own food.

So I live on living things instead, It may be a leaf, a fruit or some bread.
When I'm in Penicillin, I help you get well. I am in blue cheese, I taste really swell.
I'm made up of branches of hyphae they say. When I am in bread mold, I'll grow in this way.

Inside the bread, my rhizoids will grow. And above the bread, my stolens will show.

Then my upright hyphae at their ends will hold. A tiny spore case to make more molds.
To reproduce asexually is not hard for me. My spore cases open and set my spores free.
The wind will carry them to every open space. They will grow if they land on a suitable place.

ASEXUAL REPRODUCTION -
SPORES RELEASED

But sexually, I won't reproduce quite the same.
For I have a plus and a minus strain.
When these cells unite, reproduction comes
true. They form a fertile egg called a zygote to
you.

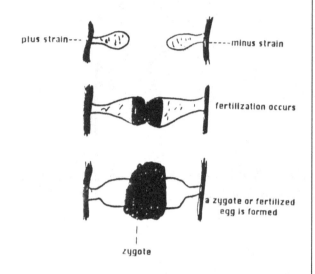

plus strain--- ---minus strain

fertilization occurs

a zygote or fertilized
egg is formed

zygote

So next time you buy the food that you eat.
Look at your ham, your break or your sweets.

If your food isn't dry or if it's not cold. I may be
with it. My name is mold.

Make a list of how long it takes for mold to form on food. Use bread, yellow cheese, a tomato, a pepper and other foods you can think of. Make a chart of information and fill in how long it took to form mold. Which was the fastest? How can you keep food from getting mold on it? Use the chart below.

Put foods in plastic bags and observe them.

Foods Refrigerated	Days & Hrs. for Mold	Foods – Not Refrigerated	Days & Hrs. for Mold
bread			
yellow cheese			
tomato (half)			
a pepper			

_____formed mold the fastest in _____days_____hrs.

_____formed mold the slowest in_____days_____hrs.

Write a poem or a story about your foods in your experiment with mold. Write it below.

What kind of plant am I?

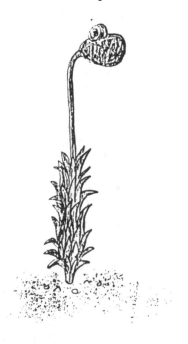

WHAT AM I ??????

In cracks between sidewalks. In moist ground under trees. These are some places you may find me.

I'm all over the world. I'm even in France. I look like a green carpet, but I'm a clump of green plants.

Each of my plants have their own tiny stems.
With a cluster of leaves encircling them.

I don't have true roots under my stem, My
rhizoids serve the purpose, instead of them.

At the base of my plant, my rhizoids are found.
They'll anchor my plant- right to the ground.

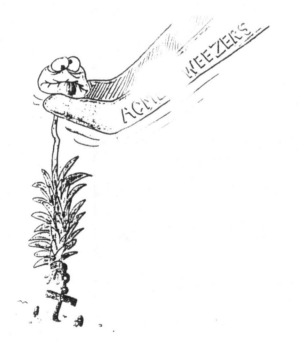

They look so small. You should know what
they're worth. They absorb water and minerals
right from the earth.

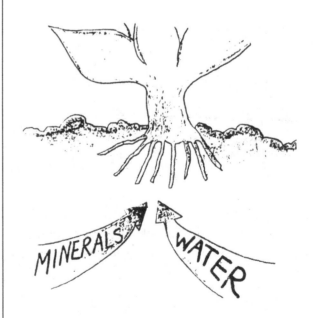

Small threadlike structures are just under my stem. They're called protonema. I have lots of them.

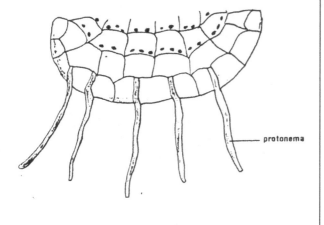

protonema

I'll make my own food with the chlorophyll in them. And from these structures, new buds will begin.

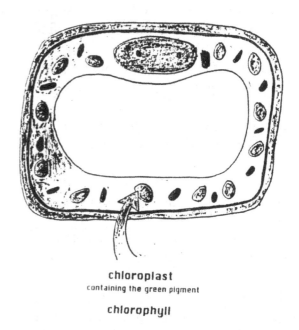

chloroplast
containing the green pigment

chlorophyll

Sexual and asexual is my reproduction game. Alternation of generations is its proper name.

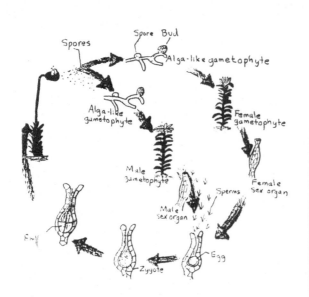

Spores

Spore Bud

Alga-like gametophyte

Alga-like gametophyte

Female gametophyte

Male gametophyte

Female sex organ

Sperms

Male sex organ

Egg

Zygote

If you don't know me yet, I guess you just lost. What else could I be – But a little old moss.

WHAT KIND OF PLANT AM I?

WHAT AM I?

In cracks between sidewalks, in moist ground under trees,
These are some places where you may find me.

I'm all over the world. I'm even in France.
I look like a green carpet but I'm a clump of green plants.

Each of my plants have their own tiny stems,
With a cluster of leaves encircling them.

I don't have true roots under my stem.
My rhizoids serve the purpose, instead of them.

At the base of my plant, my rhizoids are found.
They'll anchor my plant right to the ground.

They look so small. You should know what they're worth.
They absorb water and minerals right from the earth.

Small threadlike structures are just under my stem.
They're called protonema, I have lots of them.

I'll make my own food with the chlorophyll in them.
And from these structures, new buds will begin.

Sexual and asexual is my reproduction game.
Alternation of generations is its proper name.

If you don't know me yet, I guess you've just lost.
What else could I be but a little old moss.

Go outside and get some moss. Look at it with a hand lens. Draw it below. Can you label some of its parts?

THE BEAN PLANT!

THE BEAN PLANT!

Did you ever plant a beat seed? Do you know just what it will need?

It needs soil, moisture, and sunlight. And the temperature around it must be just right.

AHHHH!

And then- When you put your bean seed in the ground. I'll tell you that it will do.

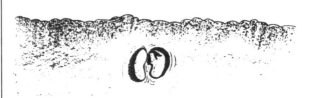

With the right temperature, soil and moisture, the seed will split in two.

And after the seed is open, the growing part begins.

On the bottom you'll see a root. On the top you'll see a stem

When it comes out of the soil, the stem can be seen. You'll see the seed case, with the seed leaves in between.

If you treat your plant right, it will grow day and night.

New leaves and flowers will come into sight.

And after the flowers, you'll feel like a winner.

When you can pick your beans and eat them for dinner.

Draw and label a Bean plant on the "big" page 111.

THE LIFE OF A PITCHER PLANT

On moist soil in the bogs of the land. You can find organisms called Pitcher plants.

It resembles a cup or a pitcher a lot. And has a green leaf with an opening at the top.

It has "hairs" on its insides which are pointed down. And it waits for an insect to come around.

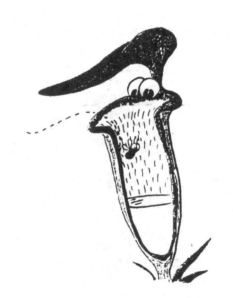

When an insect comes by and falls into its cup. The "hairs" pointing downward keep the insect from getting up.

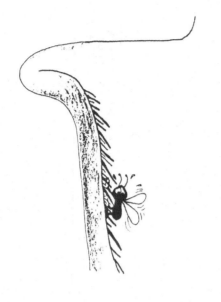

It falls into the liquid at the bottom of the cup And the enzymes in the liquid break the food up.

After the food is digested the plant remains well.
The food material is absorbed into the leaf cells.

Draw and label a pitcher plant on "big" page 111

How is a bean plant different from a pitcher plant? List them below. Use the bean plant poem and the pitcher plant poem on the previous and *following pages to help you.*

On moist soil in the bogs of the land,
Are found organisms called pitcher plants.

It resembles a cup or a pitcher a lot,
And has a green leaf with an opening on top.

It has "hairs" on its inside which are pointed down.
And it waits for an insect to come around.

When an insect comes by and falls into its cup,
The "hairs" pointing downward keep the insect from
getting up.

If falls into the liquid at the bottom of the cup,
And enzymes in the liquid break the food up.

After the food is digested the plant remains well.
The food material is absorbed into leaf cells.

Use this page for notes, drawings or your poems or songs.

THE BEAN PLANT

Did you ever plant a bean seed?
Do you know just what it will need?

It needs soil, moisture and sunlight,
And the temperature around it must be right.

And then when you put your bean seed in the ground,
I'll tell you what it will do.
With the right temperature, soil and moisture,
The seed will split in two.

And after the seed is open,
The growing part begins.
On the bottom you'll see a root,
And on the top you'll see a stem.

When it comes out of the soil, the stem can be seen.
You'll see the seed case with seed leaves in between.

If you treat your plant right, it will grow day and night.
New leaves and flowers will come into sight.

And after the flowers you'll feel like a winner,
When you can pick your beans and eat them for dinner.

Draw and label a bean plant.

Draw a pitcher plant.

How are they alike and how
Are they different?

THE TEETH OF DIFFERENT ANIMALS

You can tell what an animal will probably eat – by opening it's mouth and looking at its teeth.

A squirrel has two incisor teeth, two up and two down. To eat the acorns, nuts, and fibers around.

These chisel like teeth will gnaw food on hand. The squirrel also has some back teeth to chew on some plants,

The cats teeth are adapted to grasp its prey.

To cut up its flesh before it's swallowed away

Canine teeth perform this instead. They're found top and bottom on each side of the head.

Name the four different types of teeth discussed in this poem.

1. _____
2. _____
3. _____
4. _____

What other animals have those types of teeth.

Answer these questions on the "big" page # 122

_____
_____
_____
_____
_____
_____
_____
_____

THE TEETH OF DIFFERENT ANIMALS

You can tell what an animal will probably eat,
By opening its mouth and looking at its teeth.

A squirrel has four incisor teeth, two up and two down,
To eat the acorns, nuts and wood fibers around.

These chisel-like teeth will gnaw food on hand,
And the squirrel has some back teeth to chew on some plants.

The cat's teeth are adapted to grasp its prey,
To cut up its flesh before it's swallowed away.

Canine teeth perform this instead.
They're found top and bottom, on each side of the head.

THE TEETH OF FISH

Deep in the sea, it preys upon other animals within reach.
It has a large mouth and large pointed teeth.

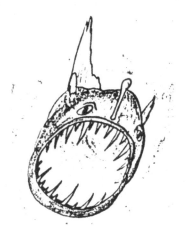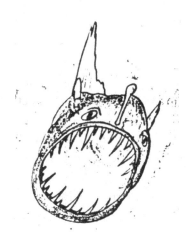

Animals are attracted to it and soon meet their deaths.
As they swim towards light-producing organs on its head.

THE TEETH OF FISH

Name the four different types of teeth in this poem.

1._____

2._____

3._____

4._____

What other animals have those types of teeth?

_____

_____

_____

_____

_____

_____

_____

_____

Use this page for your notes or your own poems or songs or drawings about science.

Use this page for your notes or your own poems or songs or drawings about science.

Hawks and owls have bills that point down. Adapted to tear flesh from the prey that they've found.

But the Heron's bill is different. It's a pear shaped device.
For catching frogs and small fish- it works kind-a-nice.

As a seed eating bird- a sparrow has its place

It uses a powerful bill, which is heavy at its base.

A woodpecker has a chisel-like beak to serve all its needs.

To ferret out insects in the bark of the trees.

Draw the four types of beaks of birds.

What other birds have those types of beaks?

Draw the bill of hawks and owls.

Draw the heron's bill.

What other birds have this type of beak?

What other birds have this type of beak?

Draw a sparrow's bill.

Draw a woodpeckers bill

What other birds have this type of beak?

What other birds have this type of beak:

BEAKS OF BIRDS

Hawks and owls have bills that point down,

Adapted to tear flesh from the prey that they've found.

But the heron's bill is different. It's a pear-shaped device,

For catching frogs and small fish. It works kind-a-nice.

As a seed-eating bird, a sparrow has its place.

It uses a powerful bill which is heavy at its base.

A woodpecker has a chisel-like beak to serve all its needs,

To ferret out insects in the bark of the trees.

Write a poem about your favorite bird, or one you see a lot in your neighborhood.

STARFISH

A starfish doesn't eat fish or ham.

A starfish's meal consists mostly of clam.

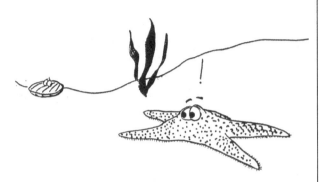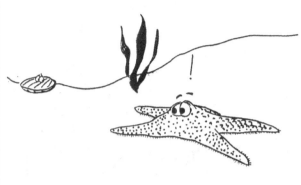

When it finds a clam on the bottom of the sea.

It wraps around it and pulls with its tube feet.

The clam is strong when the battle starts.

Bulled it soon grows weak and is pulled apart.

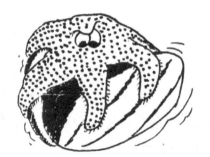

The starfish is adapted to obtain food a certain way.
Its stomach is forced through its mouth opening – to digest its prey.

.

The stomach will wrap around this fleshly food.

To digest the clam – enzymes are used.

And after its finished eating the food on hand.

It will pull away and look for more clams.

STARFISH

A starfish doesn't eat fish or ham.
A starfish's meal consists mostly of clam.

When he finds a clam on the bottom of the sea,
It wraps around it and pulls with its tube feet.

The clam is strong when the battle starts,
But it soon grows weak and is pulled apart.

The starfish is adapted to obtain food a certain way.
Its stomach is forced through its mouth opening,
To digest its prey.

The stomach will wrap around this fleshly food.
To digest the clam, enzymes are used.

And after its' finished eating the food on hand,
It will pull away and look for more clams.

Draw a starfish and write a poem or story about it.

THE GRASSHOPPER

Some grasshoppers are green and some appear red.
They have a thorax, abdomen and head.
As small as they are, they really do well.
They have little antennae to feel and to smell.

I am an insect. I've got six legs you see,
And three parts to my body. I am an insect.

And when their vision is simple as pie,
They're looking at you through three simple eyes.
But the part where hundreds of images lie,
Is known to the grasshopper as the compound eye.

The compound eye aids in detection,
Of food and also serves for protection.
And eating food is easy to work out,
Because of strong jaws and the parts of its mouth.

And through the fields, its journey will ring,

Using three sets of legs and two sets of wings.

And a grasshopper can never be bothered in the day,

Because of strong legs, which help it jump away.

I am an insect. I have six legs you see,
And three parts to my body. I am an insect.

THE GRASSHOPPER

Some grasshoppers are green and some appear red.
They have a thorax, abdomen and head.

As small as they are, they really do well.
They have little antennae to feel and to smell.

Chorus: I am an insect. I've got six legs you see,
          and three parts to my body. I am an insect.

And when their vision is simple as pie,
They're looking through three simple eyes.

But the part where hundreds of images lie,
Is known to the grasshoppers as the compound eye.

Chorus: I am an insect. I've got six legs you see,
          and three parts to my body. I am an insect.

The compound eye aids in detection
Of food and also serves for protection.

And eating food is easy to work out,
Because of strong jaws and the parts of its mouth.

Chorus: I am an insect. I've got six legs you see,
          and three parts to my body. I am an insect.

And through the fields its journey will ring,
Using three sets of legs and two sets of wings.

And a grasshopper can never be bothered in the day,
Because of strong legs which help it jump away!

Chorus: I am an insect. I've got six legs you see,
          and three parts to my body. I am an insect.

Write a poem or story about another type of insect. You could write about butterflies, bees, a praying mantis, fireflies, house flies, or your favorite type.

Let's see how much you remember.

Fill in the blanks from memory.

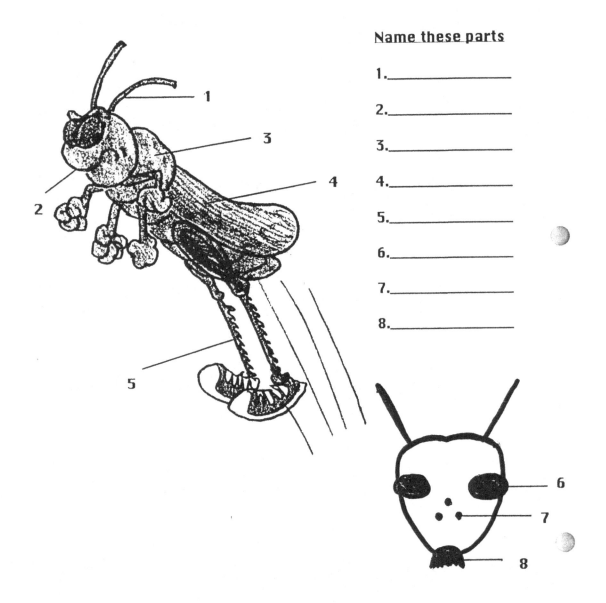

Name these parts

1._____

2._____

3._____

4._____

5._____

6._____

7._____

8._____

Draw the grasshopper from memory and label its parts.

THE INCHWORM

by
Mr. A. Musmanno
Coordinator of Science K-6

Chorus: We've got an inchworm.
We've got an inchworm.
It was hanging from the tree outside.
We've got an inchworm.
We've got an inchworm.
And it's moving and it's alive.

We wonder how many legs an inchworm has
to help it bend and move.
And what will it be when it grows up,
and will it be real soon?

CHORUS

We can see its legs with our hand lens,
and it seems that there are six.
And the library says as an adult,
the Butterfly Moth is it!

CHORUS

An inchworm is the larval stage,
the pupal stage is next.
Then it becomes a Butterfly Moth,
an adult at its best!

CHORUS

Well it's got six legs and as a moth
it will have three body parts.
That's a clue for me and you,
it's an insect from the start.

CHORUS

Well here's the way it lives its life,
it eats leaves without a halt.
It goes from egg – larva – pupa too,
and then a moth adult.

CHORUS

In April or May in New Jersey, there are a lot of inchworms hanging around. Catch some. Put them in a jar or tank with leaves and watch them. Watch how they move and change into pupa. Use a magnifying hand lens and draw then below. Write your own poem or song about them.

"THE LITTLE CRITTER"

by Mr. Musmanno
Coordinator of Science K-6

M is for my color of yellow or light brown.

E is for my every part and where my parts are found.

A is for my antennae – two – for touch and smell.

L is for me, a larva, moving very well.

W is saying watch – my six legs and three body parts.

O is for obviously, I'm an insect from the start.

R is for remember my egg – larva – pupa – adult too.

M is for my life cycle and insect parts for you.

Put them all together – it's me, a mealworm, and my larva parts.

And my head, thorax and abdomen too, are my 3 body parts. So 6 legs and 3 body parts make me an insect *see*!
And my life, egg – larva – pupa too and a beetle naturally.

My life cycle and body parts are shown below on my insect chart.

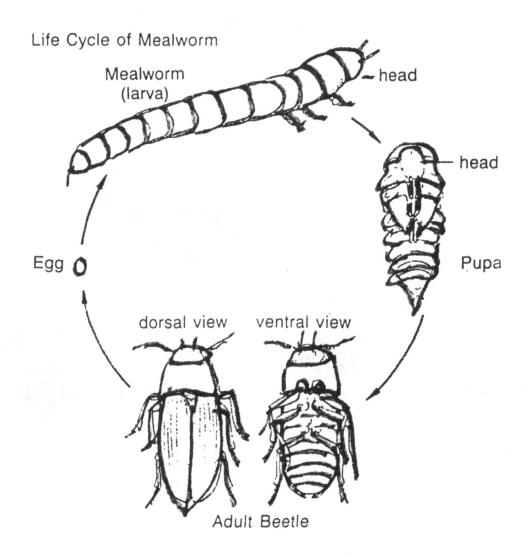

Life Cycle of Mealworm

SOCIAL INSECTS

THE ANT

146

SOCIAL INSECTS
THE ANT

Ants, bees, wasps and termites, their neighbors. Are insects which show us social behavior.

We can't look at them all. There's so many. We can't. So let's use an example like the ant,

Each ant has a special job to do. Ants live in a colony. It's like a community to you

The biggest person in your town is the mayor you see. And the queen is the "biggest in the ant colony
For every ant in the colony – she is the mother. She's two or three times bigger than all the others.

Having laid her eggs, she still has no home.

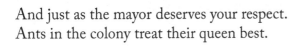

And just as the mayor deserves your respect. Ants in the colony treat their queen best.

She waits patiently and takes care of her eggs.
She moves around a little and moves her legs.

And while she's waiting, through stages they will go.

From egg—larva- pupa – to adults – they will grow.

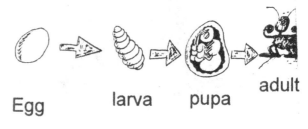

And just as you do chores around your place.
Each ant has a special job it must face.

Just as policemen enforce the laws in your town.
And wear hats and uniforms to show they're around.

Some ants have bigger heads than others do.

They're known as soldier ants for me and you.

These females guard the colony from the enemies they fear.
They help dig out the tunnels and always stay near

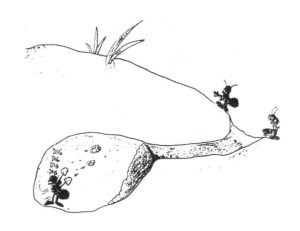

Just as people in your community work to build
  your town,
The workers in a colony work all day round.
They are also females and have a special job to
  do.
They dig out a home, to last the colony
  through.
They dig out the tunnels everywhere they go.
And dig the queen's quarters, a special room
  you know.
And they dig all day, moving their legs.
Some stay with the queen and care for her
  eggs.
And after they build a nest, suitable and neat,
They go out and get food, so others may eat.

(see next page)

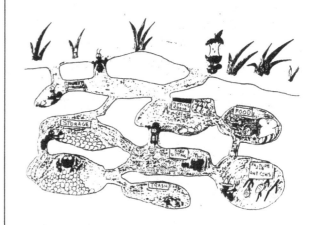

Near the queen's quarters there is a special room. Filled with winged males and females, the future brides and grooms.

And one time it will happen,, day or night, They'll take off in a marriage flight.

And while they're flying way up there. Male and female reproduce in the air.

And after reproduction the female flies.

And after reproduction the winged male dies.

And now her royal majesty
Lands and bites the wings
Off her sides,

She must start a new colony
Never again will she fly.

She'll crawl under a rock in the earth all alone.

Lay her eggs and wait till they
Build her a home,

SOCIAL INSECTS – THE ANT

Ants, bees, wasps, and termites, their neighbors,
Are insects which show us social behavior.

We can't look at them all, there's so many, we can't.
So let's use an example, like the ant.

Each ant has a special job to do.
Ants live in a colony, like a community to you.

The biggest person in your town in the mayor, you see,
And the queen is the biggest in the ant colony.

For every ant in the colony – she is the mother.
She's two or three times bigger than the others.

And just as the mayor deserves your respect,
Ants in the colony treat their queen best.

In the beginning the queen will sit all alone.
Having laid her eggs, she still has no home.

She waits patiently, takes care of her eggs.
She moves around a little and moves her legs.

And while she's waiting, through stages they will go.
From egg – larva – pupa – to adults they will grow.

And just as you do chores around your place,
Each ant has a special job it must face.

Just as policemen enforce the laws in your town,
And wear hats and uniforms to show they're around,
Some ants have bigger heads than others do.
They're known as soldier ants for me and you.

The females guard the colony from the enemies they fear.
They help dig out the tunnels and always stay near.

Just as people in your community work to build your town,
The workers in a colony work all day round.

They are also females and have a special job to do.
They dig out a home to last the colony through.

They dig out the tunnels everywhere they go,
And dig the queen's quarters, a special room you know.

And they dig all day, moving their legs.
Some stay with the queen and care for her eggs.
And after they build a nest, suitable and neat,
They go out and get food so others may eat.

Near the queen's quarters there is a special room,
Filled with winged males and females, the future brides and grooms.

And one time it will happen, day or night.
They'll all take off in a marriage flight.

And while they're flying way up there,
Male and female reproduce in the air.

And after reproduction, the female flies.
And after reproduction, the winged male dies.

And now her royal majesty lands and bites the wings off her sides.
She must start a new colony. Never again will she fly.

She'll crawl under a rock or in the earth all alone,
Lay her eggs and wait till they build her a home.

ECOLOGY POEMS

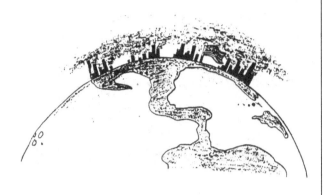

Three blind mice, three blind mice. See how they run,
See how they run.
They run crooked as you can see. They ate the corn sprayed with DDT.
This is the last day for the family. Of three blind mice, three blind mice,

Twinkle, twinkle, little star.
How I wonder where you are.
The books I've read had said you're there. But that was before the polluted air.

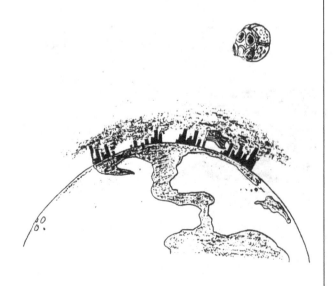

This world to me is just confusin"
Filled with people disillusioned.

Filled with people throughout the land,
Who just don't seem to understand.

The phosphates from your washing machines –
are polluting all my lakes and streams.

They're throwing paper on my street, Polluting
fish that I might eat,

With your oil spills and atomic blasts- Just
how long can our wildlife last?

You pollute my land and air without hesitation.

Even killing the eagle- the symbol of our nation.

Listen to what I say. Please understand !

I don't like my earth this way. I love my land.

Save my air so I may breathe, Save my food so I may eat.

Save the fish so they may stay. Save your land in every way.

As the garbage piles on my street. The world becomes a garbage heap.

As you throw Waste in land water and air.

I just want to tell you. I CARE!

Write your own ecology poem. You can write about oil spills, recycling, atomic blasts, soil conservation or anything that you feel will help ecology in your neighborhood.

Fill in what you think they're saying about ecology.

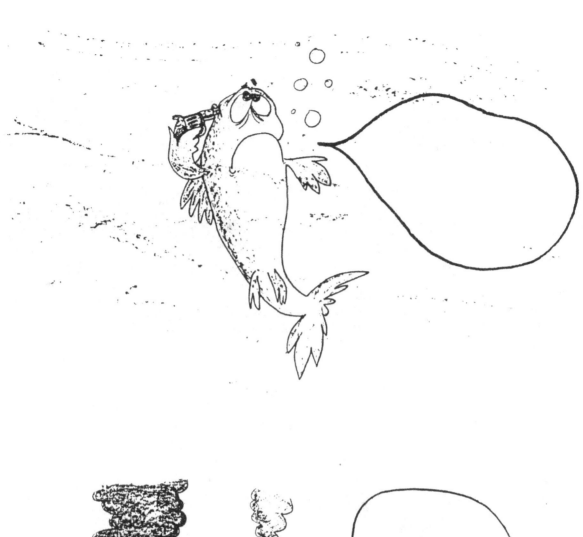

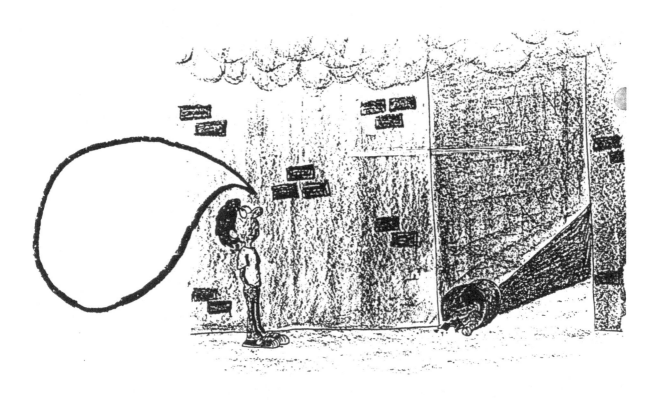

Make your own cartoon about ecology.

Take this page out. Fold in half one way and then the other. You will have a card to fill in and send. (Next page also)

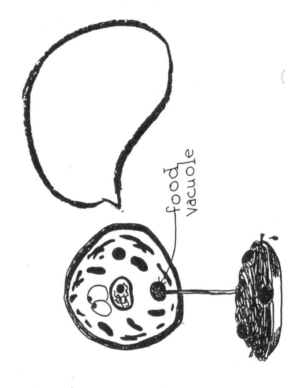

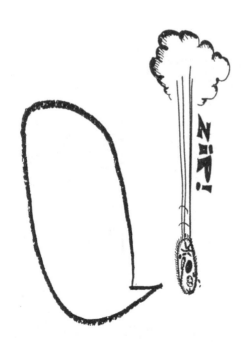

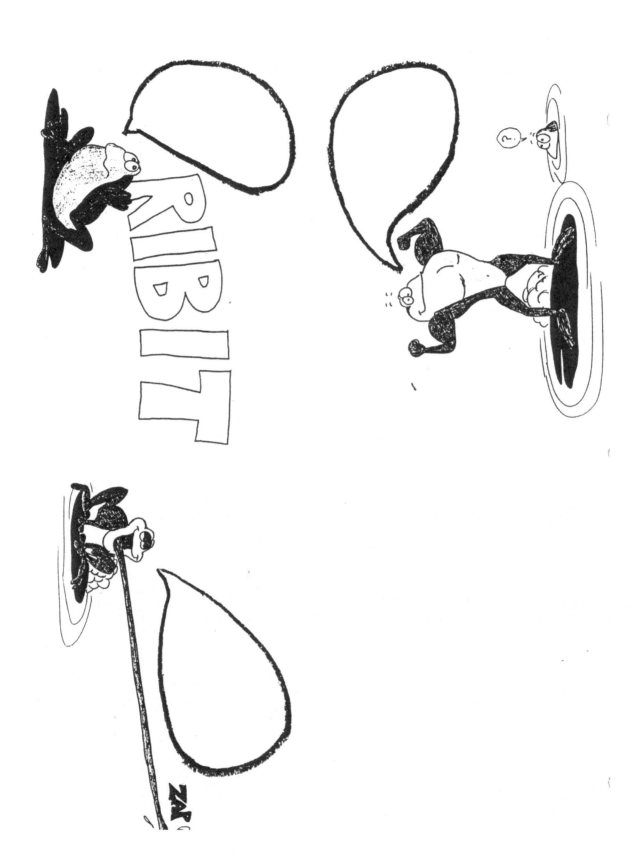

FOOD TESTS

To test for a starch you'll
Have an easy time. All you
Need is a drop of Iodine.

Put a drop on the food
And you've made a Good
Start. If that part turns
Blue-black- It's a starch

FOOD TESTS

FOOD TESTS
(See illustrations on following pages)

There are four different types of food you've seen.
Sugar, starch, fat and of course protein.
To tell the difference between each one,
There are different tests which can be done.

To test for a starch, you'll have an easy time.
All you need is a drop of Iodine.
Put a drop on the food and you've made a good start.
If that part turns blue-black, your food is a starch.

To test for sugar, Benedicts Solution is used.
Add some in a test tube along with the food.
Heat the two, look for a change.
If the food turns orange, sugar's its name.

A paper bag starts the test for a fat.
Take the piece of food and rub it on that.
If this spot becomes transluscent, light will almost pass
    through.
This will prove that the food is a fat for you.

To test for a protein, a test tube is used.
Add a bit of nitric acid and put in your food.
Heat this tube and add ammonium hydroxide.
If your food is protein. it will turn orange inside.

A paper bag
Starts the test
        for a fat.

If this spot becomes
Transluscent, light
Will almost pass   ies
Through.   it

This will prove that the
Food is fat for you.

the

To test for sugar, Benedicts
Solution is used. Add some in
A test tube along with the
Food.

Heat the two. Look for a
Change. If the food turns
Orange, Sugar's it's name.

To test for a protein
A test tube is used.
Add a bit of nitric
Acid and put in your food.

Heat this tube
Carefully and add
Ammonium
Hydroxide,

If your food is a protein,
It will turn orange
Inside.

Put a piece of bread, cheese, paper, candy, potato, apple, banana, some corn oil and some flour in front of you on a table. Use iodine, Benedicts Solution (the drug store has it) and a paper bag to test whether they are starches, sugars or fats. If they are not any of these, they are protein. Fill in the char below. Check in the box.

Item Used	Starch	Sugar	Fat	Protein
Bread				
Cheese				
Paper				
Candy				
Potato				
Apple				
Banana				
Corn Oil				
Flour				

Write a poem about what you did and your results.

Use this page for notes, drawings or your poems or songs.

CLASSIFICATION OF VERTEBRATES

The things that are held within this poem—are only the animals which have backbones.

All of these animals are alike in one way. They're all in the phylum of vertebrates.

But each animal is different. Let's begin.

Can you guess which class each animal is in.

CLUES:

(for suspect #1)

WARM BLOODED.
NOT STRANGE.
NOT AFFECTED IN
TEMPERATURE CHANGE
HAIR COVERED.
LUNGS FOR AIR

I'm warm blooded. I'm not a strange.
I'm not affected when temperature change.
Hair is the outer covering of me.
I have lungs so I may breathe.
If you don't know me yet, I'll give you some help.
Look in a mirror. Look at yourself.

What am I?

CLUES:

(for suspect # 2)

WARM BLOODED.
LUNGS FOR AIR.
FEATHERS FOR
COVERING.

I'm also warm blooded, but I don't look the same.
Try to guess my class or my name.
I also have lungs so I may breathe,
But I have feathers on the outside of me.

What am I?

CLUES:

(for suspect # 4)

COLD BLOODED.
HEAD AND TAIL.
COVERED WITH
PLATES AND SCALES.

As the temperature around me goes up or down,
My body adjusts to the temperature around.
For I am cold blooded, inactive in cold weather.
That should help you know me better.
I have a head and I have a tail.
My body is covered with plates and scales.

What am I:?

CLUES: COLD BLOODED.
                SCARES GIRLS.
(for suspect # 4) THIN SKIN. NOT MEAN.
                YOUNG HAVE GILLS.
                OLD HAVE LUNGS.
                JUMPS

I'm also cold blooded. I make girls scream.
My skin is thin. I'm really not mean.
I breathe through gills when I am young.
When I grow old I may develop lungs.
If you're a little confused, I'll give you a clue.
If you walk towards me, I might jump at you.

What am I?

CLUES: LIVES IN WATER.
                COLD BLOODED.
(for suspect # 5) SMART.
                MANY BONY PARTS.
                BREATHES WITH GILLS
                AND LUNGS.
                PREY OF BOYS.

I live in the water. I'm cold blooded and smart.
My skeleton contains many bony parts.
I breathe through gills and sometimes lungs.
Boys try to catch me when they're young.

What am I?

CLUES: GILLS UNCOVERED.
                CARTILAGE SKELETON.
(for suspect # 6) SALT WATER HOME.
                FEARED AT BEACH.

I have gills, but no gill covers.
How am I different from the others?
My skeleton's of cartilage, not of bone.
Salt water is my only home.
I'll give you a clue if my name's out of reach.
People are afraid of me when they swim at the beach.

What am I?

CLUES: FISHLIKE.
                NO TRUE JAWS.
(for suspect # 7) NO FINS.
                CARTILAGE SKELETON.
                DEVELOPS GILLS

I'm a fishlike animal if that gives you a hint.
I don't have true jaws or any paired fins.
My skeleton is cartilage. I develop gills.
Try to guess me, if you will.

What am I?

Write your own classification poem about birds, mammals, different types of dogs or cats, fish, sharks, reptiles, amphibians, or animals without backbones. Have fun!

CLASSIFICATION OF VERTEBRATES

The things which are held within this poem,
Are only the animals which have backbones.
All of these animals are alike in one way.
They're all in the group of vertebrates.
But each animal is different. Let's begin.
Can you guess which class each animal is in?

I'm warm blooded. I'm not strange.
I'm not affected when temperatures change.
Hair is the outer covering of me.
I have lungs so I may breathe.
If you don't know me yet, I'll give you some help.
Look in the mirror. Look at yourself.   What am I?

I'm also warm blooded but I don't look the same.
Try to guess my class or my name.
I also have lungs so I may breathe,
But I have feathers on the outside of me.   What am I?

As the temperature around me goes up or down,
My body adjusts to the temperature around.
For I am cold blooded, inactive in cold weather.
That should help you know me better.
I have a head and I have a tail.
My body is covered with plates and scales.   What am I?

I'm also cold blooded. I make girls scream.
My skin is thin. I'm really not mean.
I breathe through gills when I am young.
When I grow old I may develop lungs.
If you're a little confused, I'll give you a clue.
If you walk towards me, I might jump at you.   What am I?

I live in the water. I'm cold blooded and smart.
My skeleton contains many bony parts.
I breathe through gills and sometimes lungs.
Boys try to catch me when they're young.   What am I?

I have gills but no gill covers.
How am I different from the others?
My skeleton's of cartilage, not of bone.
Salt water is my only home.
I'll give you a clue, if my name's out of reach.
People are afraid of me when they swim at the
beach.   What am I?

181

I'm a fishlike animal, if that gives you a hint.
I don't have true jaws or any paired fins.
My skeleton is cartilage. I develop gills.
Try to guess me if you will.

Use this page for your notes or your own poem or song or drawing about Science from what you've learned.

M & M'S

by

Mr. A. Musmanno

@ 1989 A Musmanno

When I observe, I look.
When I compare, I look for different and alike.
When I infer, I use my past experience book.
When I predict, I try a good guess that's wrong or right.

I have to infer or remember my past with M & M's.
Without opening a pack, how many are there of them?
How many are orange, yellow, red or green?
How many Blue or dark brown will be seen?

And which color is there most of in each pack? _____

And which color is there least of in that little sack? _____

I have to remember that the number that I predict in each pack,
Has to be the number total for each color in the M & M sack.

Now that I've finished predicting,
I can open the sack.
And find the actual numbers,
And compare and look back.

I remember the past,
And the joy M & M's spread.
Even if I'm wrong,
I can eat them, they said.

If you're allergic to chocolate,
use Dots or bags filled with
spice candles or jellybeans to
observe, compare, infer and
predict.

You can also use packages of dots, spice candies, jellybeans, or a package of. skittles (especially if you're allergic to chocolate). If you're not allergic to chocolate you can even use M&M peanut packages and other types of M&M's. Try and write a poem or song about your new lab with the above candies!!

M & M's LAB
USING THE SKILL OF INFERRING TO PREDICT

M & M's RECORD SHEET
ACTIVITY 2-1 WHAT'S IN A BAG OF M & M's?

Objective

Participants will be able to set up cooperative task groups to distribute, use and collect manipulative science materials in a "hands-on" lesson.

Fill in your group's prediction and then open your package and count the number of M & M's to find the actual data.

	Prediction	Actual	How Many + or -
How many M&M's are in your package?			
How many M&M's are the new blue?			
How many M&M's are green?			
How many M&M's are orange?			
How many M&M's are yellow?			
How many M&M's are light brown?			
How many M&M's are dark brown?			
How many M&M's are red?			
What is the most common color?			
What is the least common color?			

Name: _____

M & M's LAB
USING THE SKILL OF INFERRING TO PREDICT

Name: _____

Number of M & M's in pack: _____

How many are: blue _____
                      green _____
                      yellow _____
                      light brown _____
                      dark brown _____
                      orange _____
                      red _____

Most common color: _____

Least common color: _____

WHEN GIVEN PERMISSION, OPEN THE PACK.

Total number of M & M's in the pack: _____

How many are: blue _____
                      green _____
                      yellow _____
                      light brown _____
                      dark brown _____
                      orange _____
                      red _____

Most common color: _____   How many? _____

Least common color: _____   How many? _____

ANSWERS

These are some answers for pages in the book.   Try them first before you look.

Pages 13 & 14: see poem on pages 10 and 11

Page 16 : 1. Cell membrane 2.endoplasmic reticulum 3. Mitochondrion 4 ,nuclear membrane
   5. chromosome 6.protoplasm or cytoplasm 7. Food vacuole

Page 24: See Paramecium poem on page 22

Page26: 1. Cell membrane 2.mouth opening 3. Protoplasm or cytoplasm 4. food vacuole 5.trichocyst
   6. large nucleus 7. Small nucleus

Pages 37 to 42: See Mitosis poem and drawings on pages 29 to 36

Page 43: Mitosis is the division of the protoplasm and the parts of the cell—and the exact reproduction
   of the nucleus and its parts. The phases of mitosis are : interphase, prophase, metaphase,
   anaphase, telophase to daughter cells.

Page 45: thymine, cytosine

Page 48: See DNA poem on page 44

Page 49: cytosine—guanine—adenine—thymine—adenine—cytosine

Page 62: 1. Cells with a long whip-like strand or more than one whip-like strand called flagella
   (one) Or flagellae (more than one) 2 . Euglenas 3. Paramecium 4. Cilia 5. Plant cells
   6.Amoebas 7. Plamodium vivax 8. Because of their many cilia which moved them like
   speedboats 9.they were able to move their protoplasm around each hurdle. 10. The euglenas
   –they put their flagella on the ground and pushed their cell way up in the air.

Pages 66 to 77: See the drawings on pages 50 to 61 or the directions on pages 65 & 78

Page 80: 1. The way things get their food 2. Making a copy of ones self 3.the way things move
   4. Being influenced or sensitive to something 5. Discharge of waste matter from the body
   6. Breathing 7. Taking in nutrients to make new cells 8.the act of absorbing something.
   9. Changing food so the body can use it. 10. Discharging of a substance

Page 83: (top left) motion (top right) food getting (bottom left)digestion (bottom right) secretion

Page 84 (top left) absorption (top right) assimilation (bottom left)respiration (bottom right) excretion

Page 85: ((top left) sensitivity (top right) reproduction page 189

Page 88: see answers in the 10 activities of life poem—pages 82 to 85

Page 92: see poem on page 90 or pages 94 & 95

Page 115: Use the bean plant and pitcher plant poems and information on pages 106 to 114

Page 118: 1.incisor teeth—2. chisel like teeth—3. grasping teeth 4.canine teeth

Page 126: see examples on page 125

Page 140: 1. Antenna 2. Head 3.thorax 4. Abdomen 5. Jumping leg 6. Compound eye 7. Simple eye 8. Strong mouth parts

Page 178 (top right) Mammal (dog , cats, human being etc) (bottom left) Birds (parakeets, canaries, crows, hawks etc) (bottom right) Reptiles (turtles , snakes etc.)

Page 179: (top left) Amphibians (frogs, salamanders etc.) (top right) Fish (sunfish , bass, trout, lungfish etc) bottom left—Sharks and rays , bottom right- sea lamprey